Contents

D0716080

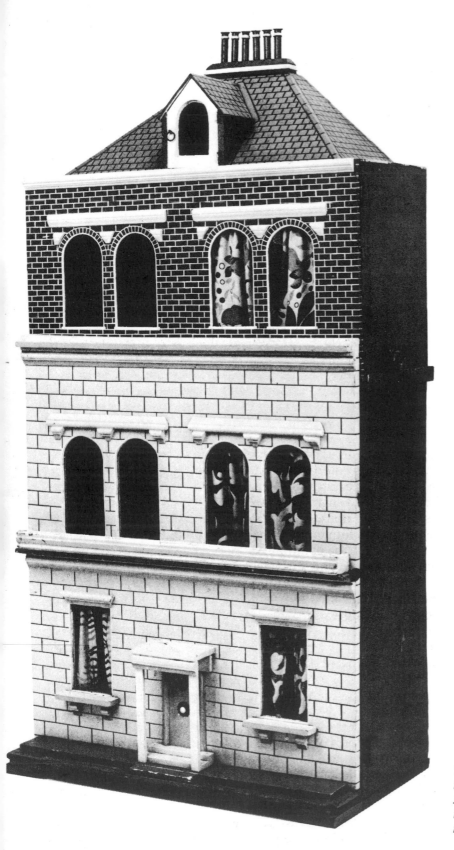

This is the family dolls' house which was given to my mother when she married. She had four sons and no daughters so I used to play with it. It was fun but the inside could have been made much more realistic.

4

Introduction

When my mother married shortly before the First World War one of her friends gave her their family dolls' house. It was intended, of course, for her first daughter, but in the end she only managed to produce four sons, of which I was the second. As a young boy I was more interested in what the house contained than in the way it had been made. Its inhabitants and the activities of their daily lives were what concerned me. The dolls themselves, their food, beds, soft furnishings and carpets: all these were more important than the fact that the rooms did not communicate with each other, that the four floors were not connected by staircases and that the front door not only failed to open but – if it had – would have hit a partition wall.

As I grew older, I became more concerned with how the building functioned and less interested in its contents. My fantasy world began to fill with the idea of making things in miniature, particularly working models. I used to dream of motor cars driven by small engines, electric trains with automatic signalling systems, dolls' houses with water supplies and rock-gardens with waterfalls and fountains. Some of these fantasies became realities, but others, like the plumbing system that I attempted to install in the dolls' house, ended in failure.

At school I was happiest in the art room and carpenters' shop, and throughout my life I have always enjoyed watching craftsmen at work and learning from them. The woodwork instruction at school was sketchy, but despite this the only school prizes I ever won were for an umbrella stand and a cupboard covered in dark brown varnish. This lack of training was in the end to prove an advantage, for it allowed whatever talent I had to develop naturally and permitted an unfettered approach to problems.

By the time I was twenty the family dolls' house was, of course, forgotten. It stood unopened, the dolls still propped up in the position they had last been moved to some years before. I made a model house for my first girl friend, but after that I decided to make real household furniture and fittings, inspired by what I saw in the more expensive shops in town and wanted, but could not afford.

When I married during the Second World War, I had little money with which to equip our house, so I made bedroom and kitchen furniture from old packing cases and secondhand wood. It taught me patience and taxed my ingenuity. Then, as my children arrived I made furniture and toys for them. After acquiring my first and only god-child, my interest in toy making took on a fresh impetus, and about twenty years ago I made her a large, open-plan dolls' house. Encouraged by the delight this gave, I began to think about making dolls' houses for sale commercially, and designed a large modern dolls' house in kit form for assembly by the purchaser. It was of limited appeal, and I still have a pile of expensive unsold parts in my workshop. I had misjudged the market and only later realised that what people want is something romantic. So I designed a little Georgian terrace house or shop, with a bow-window, a brass hand-rail to the front door, and a mansard roof. It remains a most popular design.

In my work as a family doctor, I had often seen dolls' houses no longer wanted, poised dangerously on the tops of wardrobes, stuck awkwardly in corners, sometimes consigned to the garage. They all had one feature in common: they were too big. A dolls' house should really be designed to such a size that it can share some of the space on a girl's dressing table; and if it is sufficiently elegant to be used later for haberdashery, make up or treasures when no longer wanted as a dolls' house, so much the better. It should be easy to carry about and require little by way of furnishing.

I was delighted when I was approached to write a book about my craft. My publishers considered that although dolls' history was well documented there was a need for a purely practical book for beginners on making a dolls' house, starting with first principles and showing precisely how to do it, stage by stage.

In this book we build a model of one particular house, from start to finish, and in doing so cover all the principles of design and construction needed in the building of any reasonably simple miniature house. You have the choice of building the house described in detail here, which is a good way of starting off, or of adapting the methods used to construct a model of some other house which may have more significance for the child for whom you are building it. Many people will be able to make a model of their own house – and what could be more fun for a young girl to play with than that?

As you read through the book—and *do* read through it completely before trying to build any sort of house—you will find that each stage is usually treated in two parts: the first describes the principles governing that stage and the second gives detailed instructions, with photographs, drawings and measurements, of the way in which these principles have been applied to the designing and building of the house I chose to copy. I have assumed that you have had little or no experience of carpentry and that you possess few, if any, tools. The more experienced may find the working instructions over-simplified and those with sophisticated tools will know that there are quicker ways of doing things than those described, but no-one should feel at sea if he follows the instructions and advice given.

A list of the basic tools you will need is given in Appendix I on page 77. You are likely to have some, if not all, of them already. I have occasionally made mention of one or two machine tools, in case you have them, but I must emphasise that the work can be done with simple inexpensive tools, limited skill and a modicum of patience. Machine tools save energy, do the job more quickly and, unless you are very skilled, enable you to achieve better results; but they are expensive and are not essential for our purpose. Various hints which make the work easier are given throughout the book. They may at first sight seem to make for *more* work, but I know from experience that what sometimes seems to be a long way round is quicker, easier and more satisfying in the end.

1 Planning

Planning is of fundamental importance. The degree to which the finished model is successful will depend to a considerable extent upon the care you have taken over planning it. So, although you would no doubt like to start cutting out and constructing right away, there are a number of things to be considered first.

Planning divides naturally into several parts:

1 Choosing the house (or other building) on which you are going to base the design for your dolls' house (below);
2 Taking photographs of it (page 9);
3 Deciding the scale to which you plan to build (page 12);
4 Choosing the materials from which the house will be made (page 13);
5 Designing the front of the dolls' house, on paper, and working out the dimensions (page 13);
6 Deciding how the inside is to look in general terms; and then working out how to achieve the arrangement you want, and drawing up accurate plans to enable you to do so (page 23);
7 Accurately marking up the materials to the measurements you have already worked out, ready for cutting out the 'shell' and the various pieces which together make the internal walls and floors of the house (page 34).

Only when all these stages have been completed should the construction of the house be begun. Since plans are obviously difficult to modify once the construction stage has been started, the care taken in getting them right initially is repaid many times over in being able to get on with the building of the house without having to stop to correct errors. In any case, in its own way the planning is as enjoyable as the construction.

1. Choosing your house

The first and perhaps the most important step of all is to decide which building you are going to use as the basis of your design. It is worth giving quite a lot of consideration to this. I spent part of several days choosing a house that would serve as an original for our model. I went to London on a day's holiday, taking my camera and a full roll of film. I photographed everything I thought might suit our purpose. The house I finally settled on was Charles Dickens' house.

Dickens' House is a terraced house, built at the end of the eighteenth century in a quiet Bloomsbury thoroughfare, Doughty Street, which is still a peaceful street, not far from London University. The house takes its name from Charles Dickens, the famous novelist, who wrote some of his best works, including *The Pickwick Papers*, *Oliver Twist* and *Nicholas Nickleby*, while living in it. In the summer of 1922 it was bought and preserved from demolition. Now scheduled as a building of historic interest, it contains a library and museum for the use and enjoyment of all who are interested in Dickens' life and works. In appearance it is typical of the many elegant town houses built in the early 1800's, when London was growing fast and needed graceful homes for its prospering middle class. The Georgian style, with its simplicity of design and uncomplicated façade, makes it an ideal building on which to base a first attempt at dolls' house making. Most Georgian town houses have flat roofs and are free of gables. Their shape, which resembles that of a shoe-box standing on end, is well suited to a piece of nursery furniture.

If you decide to use some building other than Dickens' House as your model, be careful not to choose one that overtaxes your skill. Sloping roofs, rounded walls, decorative mouldings and changes of plane can present problems to the most expert craftsman, and a beginner is well advised to restrict himself to a simple design. In any case, it is, perhaps surprisingly, often the simpler shapes that appeal most in the end. You may prefer to make a shop or some other type of simple building rather than a house, or to base your model either on your own house or on that in which the person you are making it for lives.

I realise that the number of basic designs which incorporate flat roofs is, of course, rather limited; although many which have some sort of sloping roof can be built without it when made into a dolls' house, and this is what I decided to do with Dickens' House. But in others the roof is an essential feature, so instructions for designing and making a pitched roof have been given on pages 73–75.

2. The photographs

When you know on which building you are going to base your design, you will need to take some photographs of it. Because the design and measurements for the front of the house will be worked out from it, it is important that you get as good a shot of the front elevation as you can. Ideally, this should be taken from directly in front of the house, and sufficiently far away from it to avoid any distortion from bottom to top. Of course, this often is not possible in a street of average width, and so you may have to

Dickens' House, Doughty Street, London. Perhaps an ideal subject to copy as a dolls' house. Its front is all on one plane, the windows are symmetrically arranged, the entrance is simple but attractive and, if you ignore the top storey, the roof can be flat.

take the house at an angle to get the whole building into the picture. The best solution may well be to ask permission to take your photograph from the first-floor window of the house immediately across the street. This is what our photographer, Clive Boursnell, did in order to get ours.

You will also need two other photographs, one which gives you an undistorted view of the whole of the ground floor, and another of the front door by itself, face on (next page). It should be possible in most cases to take these from directly in front of the building without much difficulty.

Together, these three photographs must give you a reliable guide to the main proportions of the building. They become basic to the stages which follow, and it is worth spending a little effort in order to get good ones. If you do not take photographs yourself, ask someone you know who does if they will help you. He will probably be glad to help you out.

An undistorted view of the ground floor will help you establish the true relationship between the sizes of the windows and the front door, and reveals much detail that is difficult to pick up from a photo of the whole of the front.

3. Scale

It is sensible to make your dolls' house to a scale compatible with that used for mass-produced dolls' house furniture. This is normally manufactured to one-twelfth of real size. That is to say, a cupboard 6 ft. (72 in.) high would be represented by one 6 in. high ($\frac{72}{12} = 6$). This one-twelfth scale therefore has much to recommend it, and I used it throughout the design and construction of Dickens' House. It results in a model which looks just about right for size when placed in modern rooms. You can, of course, use a different scale, but bear in mind this question of furniture and accessories.

I have used Imperial measurements throughout, since this is still common practice in both the United Kingdom and the United States, but for those who prefer to work in the metric equivalents, an Imperial–metric conversion table is given at the back of the book.

A good shot of the front door will be useful later on when you come to make the front door for the dolls' house. In this case, it provides accurate information about the panelling, the fanlight and the decorative arch.

4. Which materials are best ?

It is worth deciding early on which materials you wish to use in the construction of the model as it will directly affect some of the measurements and therefore the plans.

If you are looking for a dolls' house in a toy shop you will find that many are now made of thick card, hardboard or thin plywood. These materials are used to keep the price down and, while they make good toys, their life is likely to be short. Certainly, they will never become heirlooms. I suggest that, since you will have to use nearly as much time and energy to make a dolls' house out of these materials as you would out of something more durable, you use either best quality $\frac{3}{8}$ in. birch-faced plywood or medium density fibreboard (M.D.F.). The latter costs the same as plywood, does not warp, is better to work with and takes paint well. The only disadvantage is that you must make pilot holes when using screws in the end grain. $\frac{1}{4}$ in. M.D.F. is useful for partitions and roofs. Anything thicker is difficult to work with and unnecessarily heavy. I now use M.D.F. almost exclusively.

Although you can get ready-made windows and doors in pressed sheet metal from many do-it-yourself shops, I find them totally unsuitable and prefer to make windows either of glass or heavy plastic sheeting. Alternatively you can buy in part form, or ready-made, wooden windows with either fixed or sliding sashes. These however tend to be rather expensive, and using them denies you the satisfaction of having made the whole of the dolls' house yourself.

5. Designing the front of the house

Take a large sheet of paper (at least as large as the finished model will be) and stick it with tape on to an even larger piece of plywood or M.D.F. You are going to use this to draw the front elevation of your model. Graph paper with Imperial (or metric) size squares will make the drawing easier but you will need to use a felt pen to make the lines you draw stand out clearly. You have already decided on the scale you are going to use, and so the next stage is to use the photographs you have taken to determine the measurements for the whole model and to draw them accurately on this large sheet of paper. This is how to go about it, using the example of Dickens' House.

First, bear in mind that if a man six foot tall is to get through the front door the door has, if possible, to be at least six inches high (remembering the one-twelfth scale). I decided to make it $6\frac{1}{4}$ in. high, to give a little clearance for taller men. The height of the door in the photograph is $\frac{3}{4}$ in., or approximately one eighth the height of the door needed for the dolls' house ($8 \times \frac{3}{4}$ in. $= 6$ in.). This means that every measurement on the photograph has to be multiplied eight times to get it right for the model. (The multiplication factor will obviously vary, and depend on the dimensions of the print you are working from and what you want

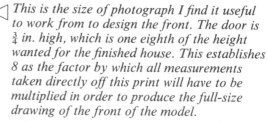

This is the size of photograph I find it useful to work from to design the front. The door is $\frac{3}{4}$ in. high, which is one eighth of the height wanted for the finished house. This establishes 8 as the factor by which all measurements taken directly off this print will have to be multiplied in order to produce the full-size drawing of the front of the model.

the overall size of the model to be. (In practice I have found it convenient to work from a print about 5 in. × 3 in.) In the photograph the width of the house at street level is $2\frac{3}{16}$ in. This means that the width of the dolls' house must be $8 \times 2\frac{3}{16}$ in. $= 17\frac{1}{2}$ in. Draw a base line close to the bottom of your sheet of paper and mark this measurement off on it. Then draw vertical lines for the sides, again using the photograph and the eight-times multiplication factor to work out how high they should be.

You will see from the photograph that the house has a top storey with dormer windows, a mansard roof and a chimney stack. I deliberately decided to leave these off because they would be difficult to model and, if included, might make the finished product look too tall. If you are designing your own model it is worth remembering that too slavish an adherence to the original can be a mistake. What you should aim for is a good overall impression. This means keeping the model as simple as possible

You use your print of the front of the building to make a full-size drawing on paper (here shown reduced). This is the first stage in designing the model. In making this drawing of the front of Dickens' House, the mansard roof, chimney stacks and dormer windows have all been omitted, without resulting in any loss to the overall design. Particularly when you are new to making dolls' houses, you should feel free to modify the original design in this way. A full page scale drawing is included for your use on page 61.

14

Although some distortion in the photographing of the front of the building is almost unavoidable, your aim should be to keep it to a minimum. This photo represents the best it is sometimes possible to achieve. It was taken from street level and fairly close up to the building. To extract useful measurements from such a shot, measure the top and bottom of the building and take an average of the two. Use the same principle for the window and door measurements. For the rest, use your eye and artistic judgment to make it look right. A less than ideal photo need not prevent you from producing a drawing like the one opposite, although you may find it easier to get the measurements right if you work from a print larger than this one.

and, if necessary, ignoring some features altogether. As an example of what I mean, I decided to give the house a straight top, cutting it off at the level of the top of the band of stonework which runs above the second-floor windows. Drawing the top at this height gives a rectangle which represents the front of the building and displays the same proportions as the original.

Next, measure how far from the edges of the house the windows, door and fanlight are in the photograph of the front, and also how big they are. Multiply all these measurements by eight (or whatever your factor is). Next, work out the sizes and positions for the windows, door and fanlight and draw them in in their proper positions within the rectangle. Draw in further lines to indicate the decorative arch round the door and fanlight, as well as the plinth at ground level, and the raised bands running across under the first-floor windows and above the top-floor windows. Your drawing of the front is now complete.

This initial drawing on paper is important, both because it is much easier to correct mistakes drawn on paper than on wood, and because it is going to be used in the design of the rest of the house. Now, therefore, is the best time to make sure it looks right to you and that it has been drawn accurately. See scale plan page 61. If you are planning to make a different building you may find it useful as an example of what you should aim for; if you are making the Dickens' House then this plan can be used in the stages which follow.

6. Some ready-made alternatives

If you want to try your hand at building a house other than (or in addition to) Dickens' House, but do not feel confident enough to go it alone entirely, you may like to consider developing one of the houses shown on the following pages. Together they illustrate ways in which various problems can be overcome, either through imagination or by simplification. Drawings have been made from the photographs, and all you need to do to get started is to make larger copies of them to the scale indicated. Remember always that you are designing a dolls' house, and not an exact replica of the original.

Little Walsingham Vicarage

*This plan shows how you can design the front
even when the view of the house is partially
obscured. A photograph of the front door and
centre section taken from the other side of the
obstructing wall gives the basic relationship of
the parts and this is then applied to the front
as a whole. I suggest you omit both the roof-
light and the addition to the right. The
moulding around the front door can also be
simplified.*

Scale: 1 in. = 5 in.

17

This is a delightful terraced house overlooking a green. It consists of three storeys with a balcony and a verandah, the roof of which you could either shape from a solid piece of wood or—perhaps even better—fashion out of sheet metal. This is quite a good illustration of the way in which it is possible to supplement the deficiencies of a photograph by guesswork and inventiveness. I have chosen to remove the chimneys and the drainpipe and to alter the front door and fanlight.

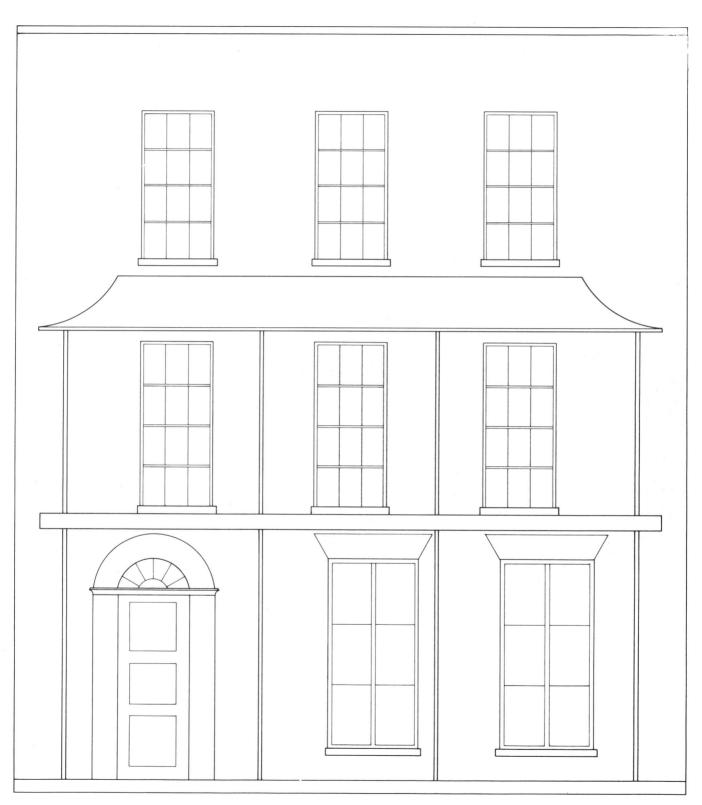

Scale: 1 in. = $3\frac{1}{2}$ in.

A slim building, showing a strong Dutch influence. Because it was tucked in between grander houses in a narrow street, it wasn't possible to get a face-on view of more than a small part of the front. However, even a photo taken at this angle can be used to produce a working elevation for the front. This building provides an ideal subject for a compact, easily made dolls' house on three floors. I suggest simplifying the windows and door and adding window boxes and a porch, though these are not shown in the drawing.

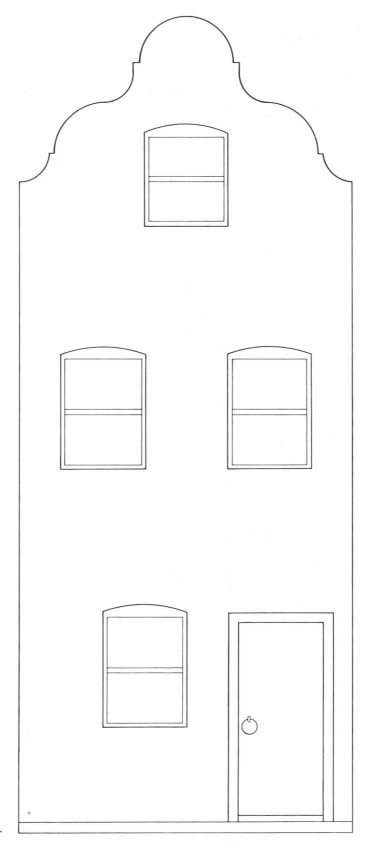

Scale: 1in. = 3in.

Scale: 1in. = 7in.

7. Designing the interior

(a) The general layout

By now you know what the height and the overall width of the building is going to be. The only external measurement still to be fixed is the depth. If you are adventurous enough to want to build a model that takes its side elevations (and perhaps even its back) from a real building, then the depth will, of course, be determined by the relationship of the side wall to the front in the original. Likewise, it must follow that the internal space available will have been fixed, in which case a certain freedom in arranging the number and the sizes of the rooms will have been forfeited: a price you may well be prepared to pay for exterior fidelity. If you are planning to build a model in which the side and/or back elevation is true to the building you have based it on, just repeat the method used for the front in order to produce working drawings.

However, most dolls' houses (and Dickens' House is no exception) have an authentic front and allow the depth to be determined by a joint consideration of the internal design and the need for the final model not to be too bulky. I recommend coming to grips first with the general requirements you want the house as a whole to meet—the number of rooms on each floor, where the stairs should go, and so on—being prepared to make adjustments where necessary to prevent the building becoming too deep. If you look at the way this question was thought about and answered in Dickens' House, then you will find it easier to come up with your own plans for any other building and will be able to take the equivalent steps towards producing working drawings.

This Norfolk Farm House has a beautifully simple elevation and an uncomplicated roof. Access to the roof space could be achieved by making two vertical cuts on the front sloping side and hinging the resulting middle piece at ridge level. You may wish to omit the centre chimney and the single storey extension to the right of the main house.

(b) The general layout in Dickens' House

Most full-size houses have rooms at the back as well as the front, separated by solid walls and communicating through doors which open and close. Stairs are often built against an outside or a party wall and rise from a hallway or from behind a small front room. It is more fun to play with a dolls' house which looks authentic inside as well as outside, but often this seems impossible to arrange. How are you going to gain access to all parts of the building if one room is set behind another? The finished model will almost certainly have to be placed against a wall, in which case it will be awkward if you have designed it to open from the back as well as the front. And an arrangement which gives access from the side not only requires extra doors but detracts from the feeling of intimacy and mystery which is a special ingredient in the success of nearly any dolls' house. What is the answer?

Whenever possible, the problem is best solved in the traditional way—by access from the front, the whole of which becomes a 'door'. This is the solution I decided to adopt in designing Dickens' House. And because I wanted rooms at the back of the

23

building as well as the front, and also wanted the eventual owner to be able to play with the stairs, I replaced partition walls with arches which allowed access to the rear parts of the house. I suspected that drawing curtains across the arched openings would be an effective way of achieving complete separation of the rooms, and in the event this has proved very successful.

The real Dickens' House has two main rooms on each of its three floors (one at the front and one at the back); a hall on the ground floor, behind which rises a staircase; and a small front room above the hall on the first and second floors.

To achieve this arrangement of rooms and staircase well in a dolls' house requires two floors, a central partition running from front to back, and two side partitions, one to the right of the central partition, the other to the left. (Throughout the book, when 'left' and 'right' are referred to assume that you are standing in the street and looking at the front of the house.) In other words the internal space of the model is divided into eight rooms, the hall and the well into which the stairs will go by the use of only five pieces of wood. These five pieces slot together to form a structure which can be inserted as a single unit into the 'shell' formed by the outer walls, by sliding it in from the front of the house.

When it comes to preparing drawings from which you can work to make these five internal pieces, the first thing to note is that two of them are plans (the first and second floors) and three are elevations (the central, left- and right-hand partitions).

Consider the floor plans first.

The inside of Dickens' House is made from only five pieces of wood: the two floors, the central partition running from front to back, and the left and right side partitions which meet it at right-angles. This view shows the side partitions partially slid into position.

(c) Working out the floor plans

If you take the external width of the house-front and deduct twice the thickness of the material you are using for the side walls, you are left with the total internal width. You have first to decide how much space is needed for the staircase well and then, bearing in mind where the windows and the front door are in the front of the house (to make sure that none of them are made to open on to the edges of partition walls) divide the space which remains in the way you consider best.

In the real Dickens' House the staircase itself is fairly narrow, but the well has to be wide enough to take two runs of stairs side by side, where each flight doubles back on itself from the half-landing, plus a small gap in between. I settled on $2\frac{3}{8}$ in. for the width of the staircase in the model, having an eye to the width of the real stairs and to the scale I was using. With a gap of $1\frac{1}{8}$ in. between two runs each $2\frac{3}{8}$ in. wide, the staircase well had to be $5\frac{7}{8}$ in. wide. From my drawing of the front I knew that the outside width of the front was $17\frac{1}{2}$ in., so the total internal width was $17\frac{1}{2}$ in. $- (2 \times \frac{3}{8}$ in.$) = 16\frac{3}{4}$ in. Taking the staircase well from that gave $16\frac{3}{4}$ in. $- 5\frac{7}{8}$ in. $= 10\frac{7}{8}$ in., and allowing $\frac{3}{8}$ in. for the thickness of the central partition wall, which I wanted to run hard up against the staircase, produced the width of the main rooms,

$10\frac{1}{2}$ in. ($10\frac{7}{8}$ in. $-\frac{3}{8}$ in. $= 10\frac{1}{2}$ in.).

The precise depth did not really seem to be dictated by anything other than the need to make sure the overall measurement was not too great and that there would be sufficient room for the flights of stairs to come forward into the hall and on to the landings above it, and still leave space for the small front rooms on the first and second floors; but the exact depth of these two rooms could be worked out afterwards. I thought the large front rooms would look good almost square, but if the back ones had been square too then the overall depth of the house would have been getting too great. These would obviously have to be shallower. After a little juggling with different combinations I settled on a depth of 9 in. for the large front room and $6\frac{3}{8}$ in. for the back room. (Because they are partly obscured by the big arches, when you look in at them from the front the back rooms seem to be bigger than they really are.) Remember that I had to allow $\frac{3}{8}$ in. for the thickness of the wood used in the left-hand side partition, and then you will see that the total internal depth came to $15\frac{3}{4}$ in. (9 in. $+ 6\frac{3}{8}$ in. $+ \frac{3}{8}$ in.).

The depth of the small front rooms (and therefore the positioning of the right-hand side partition) was influenced by the amount of room needed for the stairs. The width of the staircase well had already been decided, so it was only necessary to work out what the depth had to be. And because the depth of a staircase (front to back) and therefore the staircase well depends largely upon how high the flight is, in order to work out the depth of the well I had first to determine the height of the first and second floors. This is how I did it.

Look at the plan of the front of the house (page 35). The first floor must be high enough to clear the top of the ground-floor windows and low enough to be well clear of the bottom of the first-floor windows. I arranged for the first floor to come just above the ground-floor windows, giving a ground-floor room height of 9 in. Because first-floor rooms in Georgian houses tended to be rather grand, I made the first-floor room height in the dolls' house a little greater, $9\frac{1}{2}$ in. Having fixed on these heights, I turned to working out the depth of the staircase. (Note, by the way, that the height of the ceiling in the top-floor rooms is already fixed, determined by the overall height of the doll's house; i.e. it is the height left over after deciding on the height of the rooms on the two lower floors.)

The other factor you need to have decided is the rise (height) between two treads. In a real house this is about 7 in., and if you stick to the one-twelfth scale this means that each tread has to be approximately $\frac{1}{2}$ in. high. This was the figure I took. The height of the ground-floor rooms being 9 in. and the first-floor rooms $9\frac{1}{2}$ in., meant they required 18 and 19 treads respectively. However, one tread in each flight is replaced by a half-landing of the same thickness as a tread, so that only 17 and 18 are required.

What should the depth of each tread be from front to back? Again, in a real house it is generally about 9 in., giving a scale size of $\frac{3}{4}$ in. If I had adhered to this the total depth of the run of stairs in each flight would have been approximately $13\frac{1}{2}$ in. and $14\frac{1}{4}$ in. for the lower and the upper flight respectively. Even with each flight turning back on itself by the use of half-landings, it seemed as though such lengths were going to make the house rather too deep or else take up too much space on the landings and in the hallway, so I settled for a tread depth of $\frac{1}{2}$ in. instead.

The half-landings need to be fairly deep. I made their depths $1\frac{1}{2}$ in. Because the bottom stair of a flight rising from a half-landing rests on it, its depth is reduced on that side by $\frac{1}{2}$ in.; so at the top of a flight it is $1\frac{1}{2}$ in. deep and at the bottom of a flight it is only 1 in. deep.

Be prepared to experiment a bit to find out how many stairs there should be up to the half-landing and then on up to the first floor, and likewise from the first to the top floor. The more you have in the flight up to the half-landing the further forward into the hall will that flight extend; but the more you have from the half-landing to the full landing the deeper the staircase well will have to be. Because I wanted a fairly shallow staircase well in order to provide access to the rooms on the two upper floors (this will be explained more fully a little later on), I settled for the following arrangement:

Hall to lower half-landing: ten stairs + half-landing =
$$(10 \times \tfrac{1}{2} \text{ in.}) + 1\tfrac{1}{2} \text{ in.} = 6\tfrac{1}{2} \text{ in.};$$

Lower half-landing to first-floor landing: half-landing + seven stairs =
$$1 \text{ in.} + (7 \times \tfrac{1}{2} \text{ in.}) = 4\tfrac{1}{2} \text{ in.};$$

First-floor landing to upper half-landing: twelve stairs + half-landing =
$$(12 \times \tfrac{1}{2} \text{ in.}) + 1\tfrac{1}{2} \text{ in.} = 7\tfrac{1}{2} \text{ in.};$$

Upper half-landing to top landing: half-landing + six stairs =
$$1 \text{ in.} + (6 \times \tfrac{1}{2} \text{ in.}) = 4 \text{ in.}$$

Knowing that the long flights rising from the hall and the first-floor landing will extend approximately $6\frac{1}{2}$ in. and $7\frac{1}{2}$ in. respectively, you also know that there will be approximately $9\frac{1}{4}$ in. and $8\frac{1}{4}$ in. between the foot of the stairs and the front of the house on the ground-floor and first-floor respectively. In other words, there is, by this arrangement, plenty of depth available for the hall and the small front room in front of the stairs on the first floor. And, of course, there is no problem in fitting in the small front room on the top floor. I decided to make the depth of these small rooms on the upper two floors $5\frac{3}{4}$ in., which makes them a nice size and yet gives some space behind them before the stairs are reached.

Working out the way the stairs will be arranged has also provided you with the depths of the staircase well on the first and the top floors, respectively $4\frac{1}{2}$ in. and 4 in. (see workings above). All the measurements needed to draw up the plans for the first and top floor have now been worked out, and you should draw them full size on paper as you did the front elevation.

The floor plans for the first floor (top drawing) and second floor (bottom drawing). The shaded areas are those which will have to be cut out; the large ones become the stair well and the small slots at the edges accommodate the left-hand and right-hand side partitions. The width of a floor will of course be determined by the overall width of the house, but the depth is a matter for you to decide unless you are copying the side of a real house.

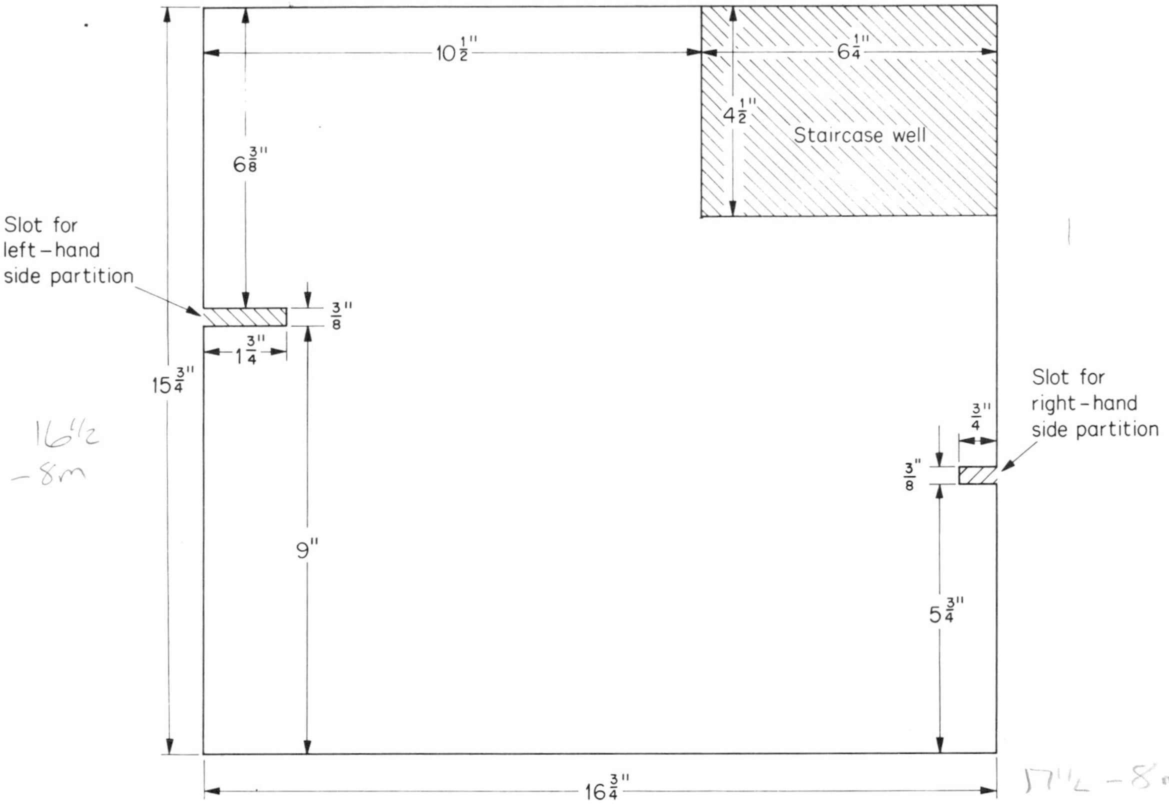

10 1/2"
6 1/4"
4 1/2"
Staircase well
6 3/8"
Slot for left-hand side partition
3/8"
1 3/4"
15 3/4"
Slot for right-hand side partition
3/4"
3/8"
9"
5 3/4"
16 3/4"

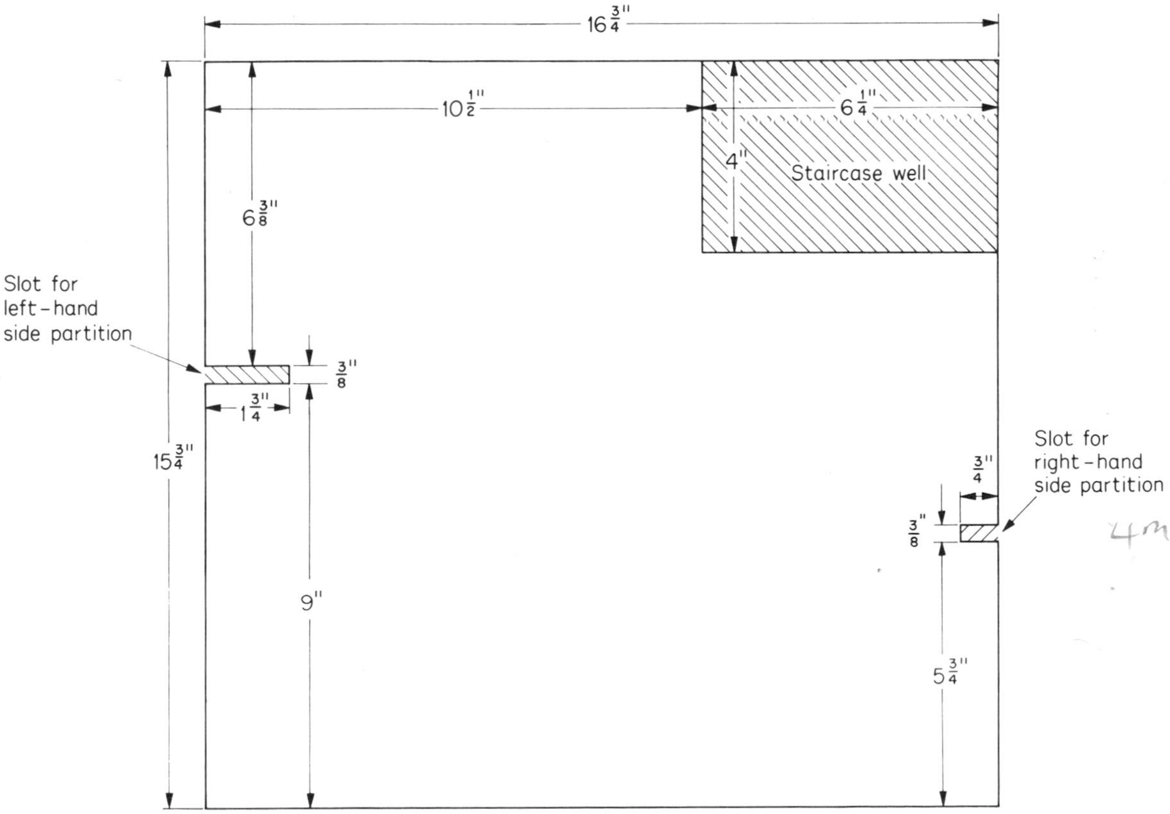

16 3/4"
10 1/2"
6 1/4"
4"
Staircase well
6 3/8"
Slot for left-hand side partition
3/8"
1 3/4"
15 3/4"
Slot for right-hand side partition
3/4"
3/8"
9"
5 3/4"

(d) Positioning of the doors and arches

Having prepared the floor plans, use them to draw up the blueprints for the three partitions. By looking at your first and second floor plans, once you have decided how many rooms you want to make out of the total floor area you can see where access will be required. If you have decided to use arches in the dividing walls then you are not bound to give all rooms a door leading directly on to the landing or hall. In Dickens' House this degree of freedom is useful, particularly in the case of the first floor, where the stairs rising from the ground floor come quite far towards the front of the house and effectively prevent the fitting in of a door from the landing into the back room. Access to this room is gained from the front room via the arch in the dividing wall.

A point worth bearing in mind is that by positioning doors near the corners of rooms you will leave maximum runs of walls free, and this is useful when it comes to arranging furniture in the finished house. It was quite easy to do this in Dickens' House by having the doors on each floor side by side in the central partition. This presented no problems on the ground floor as the staircase only occupies half the floor space, and on the first-floor landing one door serves both large rooms, so that although more space was needed by the staircase there was still plenty of room to put the door. On the top landing it was more difficult. I felt that each bedroom should have a door and this meant more space was

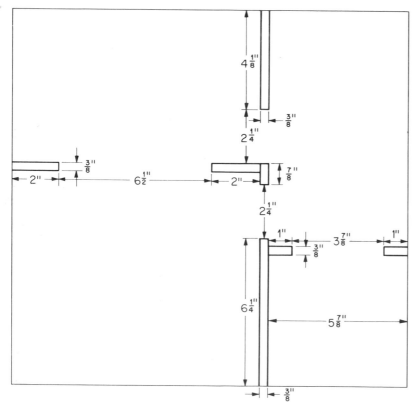

Ground floor

Make full size copies of the plans you have prepared for the first and second floors, and draw up the area of the ground floor too. Then show where the partitions will go, taking care to draw to scale the width of the material used to make them. Once you have done this you can try different arrangements for doors and arches until you are satisfied that your scheme will serve each room well. Mark these openings accurately as they will be copied on to other drawings. These three plans show the measurements I finally settled on for Dickens' House.

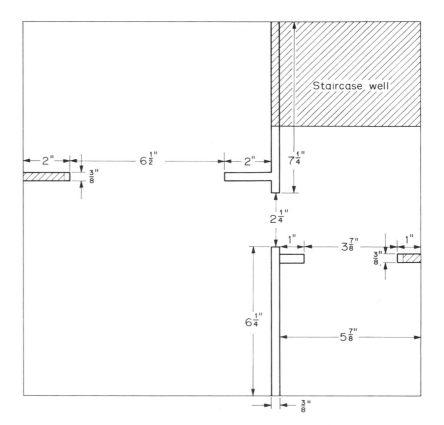

First floor

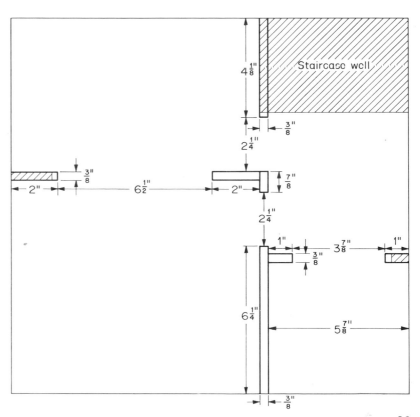

Second floor

needed on the top landing than on the one below. This was why I put more treads in the half-flight of stairs from the first-floor landing to the upper half-landing than from the half-landing up to the top floor.

You can probably see now why it is necessary to view certain stages in the designing as a whole rather than as many aspects in isolation. The measurements in the three dimensions are inevitably related to one another, and much of the skill in designing is in working coolly and steadily to convert the design which is seen three-dimensionally in one's mind into two-dimensional drawings which can be worked with.

When trying to work out the best arrangement of doors, copy the floor plans you have already prepared, and draw up a plan of the ground floor as well. (In this case, it is simply a rectangle formed by the internal measurements, $16\frac{3}{4}$ in. wide × $15\frac{3}{4}$ in. deep.) Then mark in where the partition walls will have to go in order to produce rooms to the sizes you have worked out. Next mark on these plans where the arches and doors will be. Make certain that you work accurately, for precision here will make it simple to draw the plans for the partitions.

This is the design for the central partition in Dickens' House, with detailed measurements. The dotted lines marked 'f' show where the paper was folded in order to mark off accurately where the door openings had to come, taken from the three floor-plans. The dotted line a–a has been put in to indicate where the left-hand side partition will touch it on this side, and the line b–b shows where the right-hand side partition will touch it on the other side. The long horizontal slots allow the first and second floors to be slid in from the front. They run from the front of the house until they meet the openings cut in the first and second floors (see floor plans). Making them so long means that firm support is provided for the floors along the greater part of their length.

(e) The central partition

To draw this, use a sheet of paper larger than the internal dimensions of the house from front to back. Draw the outline of the central partition, full size. (The depth is already known from the floor plans, and the height is the sum of the heights of the rooms plus the thickness of the dividing floors.) Mark accurately on this outline where the first and second floors will come. Fold the paper along the base line, which represents the ground floor, and place the folded edge along the line which represents the central partition on the ground-floor plan. Mark the doorways off with ticks on the folded plan. Re-fold the sheet for the first and second floors and repeat the marking off from the first and the second-floor plan. When you open out the sheet you will find that you have marked out the positions for all the doorways in the central partition. It remains only to decide to what height you wish to make the openings, and to draw in the necessary slots to accommodate the first and second floors. You can see from the diagram how the central partition in Dickens' House works out.

I decided not to use any interior doors, partly because they are difficult to hang and partly because I doubt whether they are really necessary, particularly as they are in the central partition and would hardly be seen. However, for those who want to use them, I have given instructions on how to fix them later in the book (page 67).

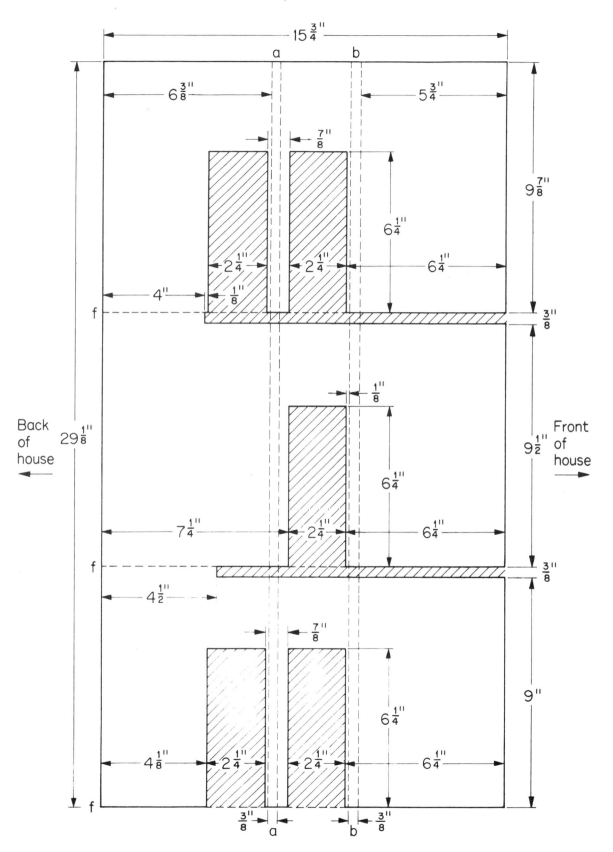

16'½ -8m

31

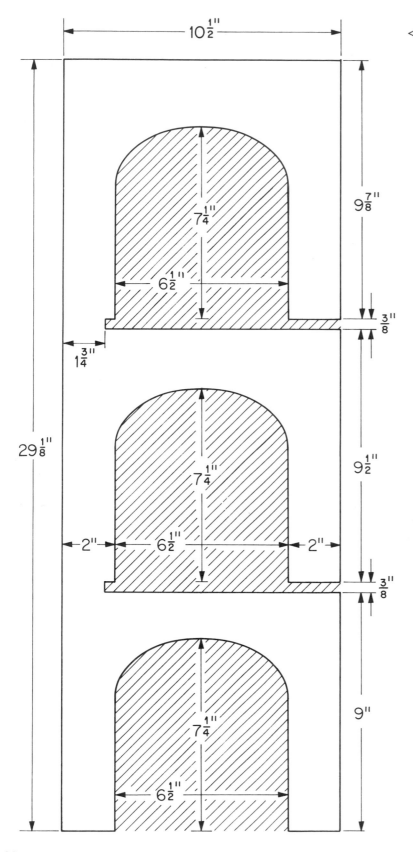

Here are the measurements for the left-hand side partition, showing the parts which have to be cut out to form the arches and the slots to accommodate the floors. To ensure the arches are symmetrical, cut a 'template' out of card, so that it is the shape of half the arch you are drawing. Put it on the centre line of the arch, then draw round it, turn it over and draw the other half of the arch by tracing round it again. The slots fit the floor plans already prepared.

The measurements for the right-hand side partition. Use a compass and pencil to make the arches, or draw them freehand.

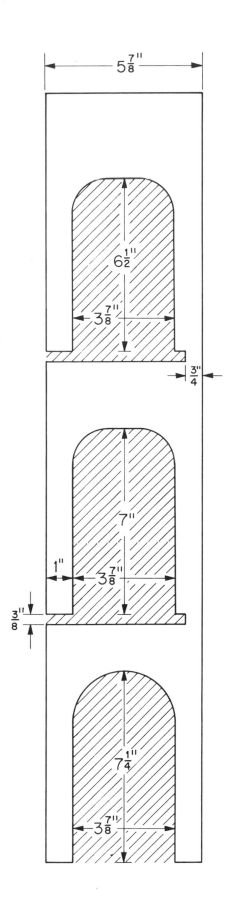

(f) The left- and right-hand partitions

Follow the same principle in drawing these as that described for the central partition. In Dickens' House the arches (which were, you remember, what I substituted for solid partition walls) lie in the same vertical line on each floor, so you need only mark them off from one of the floor plans. Note that the arches in the right-hand partition are not all the same shape. The one in the hall is half-round and is for decoration, those on the first and second floors are flat-topped with rounded corners and are meant to indicate a different function. They are room dividers like those on the left side, but are relatively wider. A narrower arch would make access to the stairs and landings difficult.

In the side partitions the width of the partition less the length of the slot equals the length of the corresponding slot in the first- and second-floor plans. The slots have to be worked out so as to give maximum support to the floors while remaining hidden when the interior is assembled. Thus in the left-hand partition the slots on the left of the arches must be very short, as must those to the right of the arches in the right-hand partition. The slots at the bottom of the other side of the arches allow the right and left partitions to be slid across the floors until they meet the central partition. The long slots in the central partition allow the floors to be slid in from the front and the central partition is supported in position by the right and left partitions.

You can draw the large arches in the left partition by eye, but in order to make them symmetrical draw half the arch on a piece of card and cut it out. Using it as a template, draw a line up the middle of the partition, place the straight vertical side of the template against this line, and draw round it. Then turn the template over to the other side of the line and draw round it again. The arches in the right-hand partition are drawn with the aid of a compass and pencil.

8. From paper to wood

You have now completed nearly all the planning which has to precede construction. Check once again to satisfy yourself that the measurements you have worked to in your drawings are correct. When you feel confident that these are right, use them to work out the dimensions for the final pieces needed for the 'shell': the base, the top, the back and the sides. There are only three points to note about these. First, it is effective to extend the base (which internally acts as the ground-floor, of course, so you can work from your ground-floor plan for this) out to the front of the house, when it serves to represent the street outside the house. Second, in Dickens' House—and, properly, in any model where the whole of the front hinges down one side—the depth of the side the front is hinged to should be less than the depth of the other side by the thickness of the closed hinge. For Dickens' House I used a 3 ft. piano hinge to support the front, and I was able to use a part of this hinge when I came to fit the small front door of the house itself. Third, the sides are the same height as the front and the internal partitions. The base and the top are the same width as the floors plus the thickness of the sides. The back fits flush with the outside edges of the sides, top and bottom.

When you have worked out the sizes of all these basic pieces, juggle them about to discover the smallest area of plywood you will need. Then lay it down and draw on to it all the plans and elevations for:

the front of the house (including the window openings and the
    front door);
the back;
the top;
the base (ground floor);
the left side;
the right side;
the first floor (remember slots and stairwell);
the second floor (remember slots and stairwell);
the central partition (slots and doors);
the left-hand side partition (slots and arches—remember the
    template);
the right-hand partition (slots and arches—compass).

(Note: the back can well be made of thinner (say $\frac{1}{4}$ in.) plywood. It only serves to seal off the back and using a thinner sheet will usefully reduce the overall weight. Decide on this before you buy your materials.)

Your careful planning is over: and the construction stage which follows will be all the easier for it.

The plans on the next two pages are for the remaining parts of the house: the simplified front, the back, the top, the base, and the left and right sides. The crosses show where holes will later be drilled to accommodate screws. The measurements and proportions shown here are for Dickens' House. When your plans have been prepared full size you can transfer them to wood prior to starting the cutting and construction of your house.

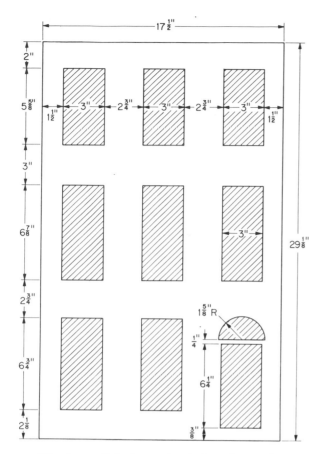

The front of the house (including the window openings and the front door)

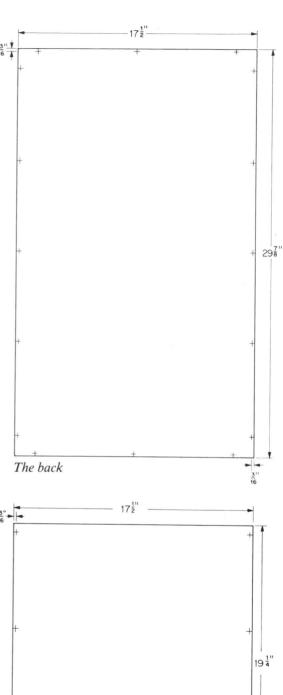

The back

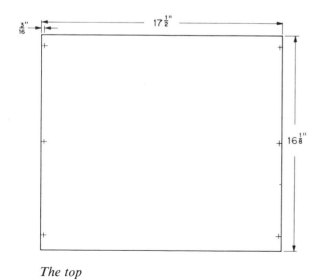

The top

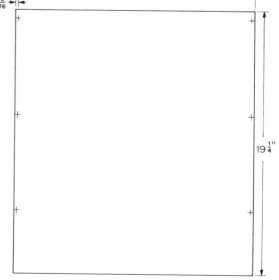

The base (ground floor)

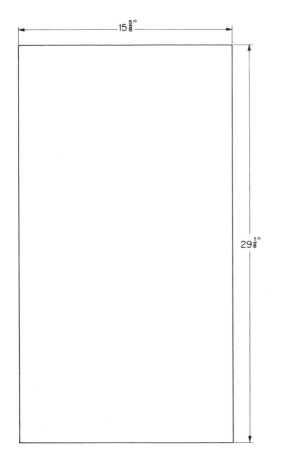

The left side

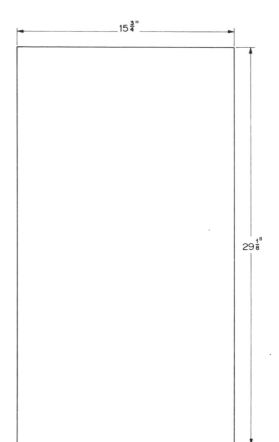

The right side

36

2 Construction

Few of us are lucky enough to have a small room or shed which is warm, dry and well-lit, and can be set aside in which to work. If you live in less than ideal conditions you can perhaps arrange for part of a room to be left undisturbed by the rest of the family while the work is in progress. A simple carpenter's bench with a vice and a sawing stool or robust low table will make the work easier, but it is possible to manage with a good solid kitchen table. Try to work in an orderly fashion, observing these simple rules:

1   Keep your working area clean and tidy.
2   Arrange your tools neatly, making racks for the smaller ones. The racks can be fixed to a wall behind your bench, or to the back of the bench itself.
3   Take the work step by step.
4   Check everything *twice* before cutting.
5   Allow yourself plenty of time.

Some aspects of the work are, by their nature, repetitive, and to do these well will require more patience than skill; but patience will be amply rewarded by the end result.

Although the construction of Dickens' House is referred to exclusively throughout this section, the principles described will obviously apply to the making of any other building designed on the lines given in Part One.

1. The front

(a) Cutting out

I always start by making the front first. Select the best area of plywood for this, remembering that it becomes a 'door' for the whole house, fitting snugly on to it when closed, and therefore needs to be warp-free. This does not apply if you are using M.D.F. It is good to get into the habit of looking carefully at the wood before marking it up and ensuring that you use the better face for the side which shows in the finished model.

Start by cutting out the whole of the front, using a ripsaw. Clean up the edges with a smoothing plane. This is made easier by the use of a power-driven circular-saw bench. You will not need to plane the cut edges if you are using M.D.F. Before you can cut out the window openings with a padsaw, you will need to drill holes in two diagonally opposite corners. These holes must

This picture shows the various stages in cutting a window out of the front. First make a pilot hole in two diagonally opposite corners, using a bradawl. Then use your brace-and-bit to drill out the corner holes (corner A). Don't forget to turn the wood over once the point of the bit has come through, and finish the hole off from the other side, otherwise you are likely to splinter the inner facing. The margins of the window are then cut with a pad saw. The best way of making a clean sharp corner is to do a reverse cut into it (as has been done in corner B).

When the window and door openings have been cut out the edges are cleaned up by sanding with a piece of sandpaper wrapped around and glued to a block of wood. Make sure that the sanding block is kept at right angles to the face of the wood.

be large enough to put the saw blade through, and are drilled with a centre bit and brace. Find the centre of the holes by drawing lines half the drill size ($\frac{5}{16}$ in. if the drill is $\frac{5}{8}$ in) away from the sides of the openings. Where they meet, make a pilot hole with a bradawl. Use this hole as a guide for the centre bit. Start drilling on the face side and when the point of the drill can be felt coming through the wood on the other side, stop drilling, take the drill out of the hole, turn the wood over, and finish drilling the hole from the back. This prevents the wood from splintering, and gives a nice clean hole. It helps to hold the wood upright in a vice while you are doing this, but you can do it almost as well with the wood placed firmly on a saw bench and steadied with your knee. Drill all the holes for all the windows, the fanlight and the door frame first and then start sawing, using the saw bench or a low table. Put the padsaw into one corner hole and cut the adjacent sides and then cut the other sides from the other hole. This operation is much easier with a powered jig saw. Before you complete your cuts, reverse the saw and cut out the little bits left in the corners. You will find it easier to do it this way rather than cutting out the middle completely and then

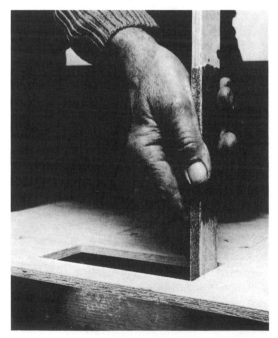

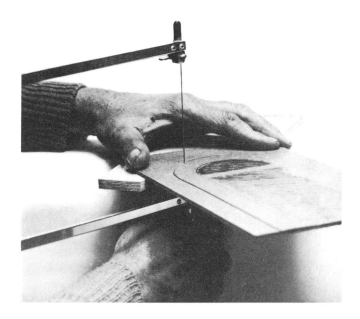
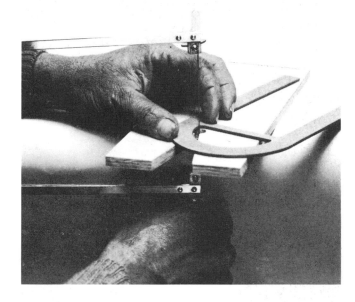

Using a fret saw, cut out the decorative arch which surrounds the front door and fanlight from a sheet of hardboard. You will have to drill a hole in the fanlight and pass the blade of the fret saw through the hole in order to cut out the fanlight.

The decorative arch is then glued in position round the front door opening.

cleaning up the corners afterwards.

If you have been very expert, a little sanding will clean up the openings you have made, but if your saw cuts have been a bit unsteady, you will need to straighten them up. To do this, glue a piece of sandpaper (see Appendix II for grade) around a block of wood. Wait until the sandpaper is firmly stuck and then use it like a nail file to smooth out any irregularities.

(b) Front door surround

Make the decorative arch around the front door in hardboard. Take the measurements from your drawing (page 35) and use a compass and pencil to draw the half-circles. The piece of hardboard you make it from should be about twice the size of the finished arch, so that you have something substantial to hold while you are cutting out. You will need a fret-saw to do the cutting: its thin blade allows you to cut curves. It is best to support the hardboard while you are cutting it. The support is quickly made. All you need to do is select a piece of wood, cut a 'V' out of one end and screw the other side to your work bench so that the end with the 'V' hangs over the edge of the bench.

Before you can start cutting the fanlight, you will have to drill a hole in it, release one end of the fretsaw blade from the saw frame, pass it through the hole, and re-secure it in the frame. When you have finished cutting the fanlight, release and remove the blade and, after re-fixing it in the frame, cut out first the door opening, and then the outside of the arch. This can be done better with a fine blade in a powered jig saw. When it is finished, glue it in position around the door opening with a suitable wood-working adhesive. Choose one which dries quickly, is clean to use, and sets hard.

(c) Stonework and plinth

The horizontal strings of stonework and the plinth at the base of the building have to be fixed next. The band at the top is made out of soft wood ($\frac{5}{16}$ in. × $\frac{3}{16}$ in. in section), cut to the same length as the width of the dolls' house front. Fix it with small panel pins (see Appendix II for size) and glue, driving the pins in with a fine nail punch. Use wood of similar section and cut them slightly wider than the width of the windows to make the window-sills. As these are short, they only need glue to fix them. The strip of wood used below the first-floor windows is made out of $\frac{7}{16}$ in. × $\frac{3}{16}$ in. section, and the plinth at the bottom out of $\frac{5}{16}$ in. × $\frac{5}{16}$ in. Both are fixed in the same way as the top band. Make a piece from $\frac{3}{4}$ in. × $\frac{3}{8}$ in. to fix to the front of the top of the dolls' house at a later stage. Fill in all nail holes with wood filler and when they have dried rub them down lightly with sandpaper.

(d) Window linings and sash bars

Next, line the window frames with strips of wood $\frac{1}{8}$ in. square. You can use balsa wood or, better, soft wood cut into strips with a circular saw bench. Balsa is easy to work, but, being very soft, bruises readily. Of course, it is not worth buying a circular bench saw, but you may know someone who has one, or you might feel inclined to hire one at the outset and to prepare these pieces along with the rest when you cut all the major parts to size. Whichever you decide to do, cut the strips of wood to length with a hobby knife and ensure they make a firm fit inside the window frames. Line the outside of the frame first, gluing the wood strip about $\frac{1}{32}$ in. back from the front of the frame. Next come the sash bars, the pieces of wood that divide the windows into small panes. You may agree that not all these need to be put in and that a single strip of wood across the middle to indicate where the upper and lower sashes meet is enough. Two pieces of wood, of equal length and half the height of the window opening less half the thickness of the sash bar, are used together as a gauge when gluing these, to ensure the bars dry in the right position. They are removed when the glue has set. Since not all the windows are of the same height (in Dickens' House, at least), you will need fresh gauge pieces for each row.

The decorative arch around the front door has already been stuck in position. If the fanlight in it is made slightly smaller than the fanlight opening in the main plywood front, there will be no need to make a fanlight lining.

Once the window openings have been lined, the central sash bar is held in place by two gauge pieces of equal length, one either side of the window opening, while it dries in position.

The front of the house is now finished with sash bars. You can also see the plinth, window sills and horizontal band of stone work beneath the first floor window fitted.

Nothing more needs to be done to the windows now until they are glazed, (see page 56). Apart from the front door the front of the house is finished.

(e) Front door

The front door is made out of wood $\frac{3}{8}$ in. thick measuring $6\frac{1}{2}$ in. × $3\frac{1}{2}$ in. Hinge it to another piece of similar thickness, using a part of the 3 ft. piano hinge you are going to use later to hang the front as a whole. Screw the narrow piece of ply to the back of the house front in such a way that the door covers evenly the hole which you have already cut for it.

If you look at the photograph of the front door on the facing page you can see that it has six panels. The best way of making them is with either thick card or very thin plywood. The latter is not easy to find and is difficult to cut, but card can be cut easily with a hobby knife. Cut it to the sizes shown in your original full-size drawing. To make sure these panels are fixed in the right position in relation to the door frame, draw the outline of the frame in pencil on to the front door when it is closed, and then unscrew the door from its hinges. Draw the position of the door panels so that they are arranged symmetrically in this pencilled frame. Glue the panels in these positions and then make a hole with a bradawl for the screw-eye-and-split-ring which serves as a door knocker. Make another hole for the door knob, which can be a brass drawer knob or large rivet, and refix the door to its hinge.

2. The interior

You have already transferred the designs for all the partitions and floors from the paper plans to wood (or other material you have decided to use in the construction of the building), and all you need do now is to cut each piece out, as you did for the front.

(a) The partitions

In Dickens' House, when you are making the partitions, start by drilling a $\frac{3}{8}$ in.-diameter hole at the inner end of each slot. Cut up to it from the outside edge, working your way around the arches as you cut towards the hole. When you have finished you will see that you have in one operation cut out the slots for the floors as well as the arches.

If you are going to fit proper doors, square the frames up with the saw in the same way as you did the window openings in the front, making reverse cuts to clear the corners. If you decide not to fix doors in the frames it looks quite effective if you leave the tops of the frames rounded.

A back view of the front door. You can see how it has been hinged to a narrow strip of wood of the same thickness, and how this has been screwed behind the opening made for it in the house front.

42

The front door, complete with panels glued in position and a screw-eye-and-split-ring serving as a door knocker. The door knob is made from a brass drawer knob or a large brass rivet.

Three types of stair tread. (a) is a simple block of wood. On (b) a lip has been formed, either by a rabbeting plane or with a circular saw; while (c) has a lip formed by gluing on a small additional strip of wood.

(b) The floors

When making the floors, cut out the overall shape first, then the slots for the partitions, and finally the staircase wells. Cut out the slots in the same way as you did those in the partitions.

3. The outside shell

Cutting out the rest of the dolls' house, the outside shell, is relatively easy. You have already marked up the five large sheets of wood needed for the sides, top, bottom and back. Select a good piece of wood for the base (ground floor), in case you want to leave the wood in its natural state.

4. Making a staircase

You will recall that in designing the interior you had to take account of the staircase and decide how many stairs you were going to have in each flight. Now you need to construct it.

Making an exact copy of a real staircase can be difficult, but there are simple ways of getting a good effect. In Dickens' House the staircase well is rather dark and any fine detail would be lost in the shadows. In many houses the assembled staircase is so little seen that you may feel that you can dispense with the banisters. (However, in case you want to make them, details of how to go about it are given on page 62. Read them before assembling the staircase.)

The stairs are made from a series of small wooden blocks or 'treads' glued together. If you intend to leave the wood in its natural state, choose something like parana pine. It has a pleasing colour and grain, a close texture and looks well if sealed with a varnish. The treads are cut from a strip of wood. They can be left as simple blocks of wood or, if you want them to look realistic, you can put a 'lip' on them. One way of doing this is to run the strip of wood through a circular saw bench, leaving a lip $\frac{1}{16}$ in. deep on one side. You can achieve the same effect with a rabbeting plane, but in either case the lips must be made at this stage. (I will not explain how to use a rabbeting plane because it is not worth

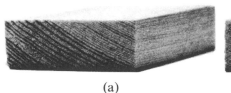

(a)

(b)

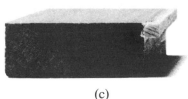

(c)

buying for this operation alone, and if you already have one you will know how to use it.) A second way of getting a 'lip' is by gluing on lengths of balsa or a harder wood (like the strips lining the windows) $\frac{1}{16}$ in. square.

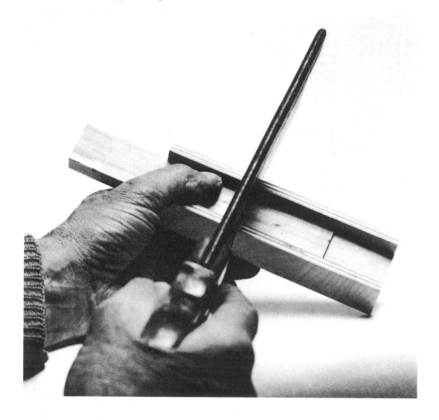

Cutting a stair tread, using a simple cutting box formed by three pieces of wood glued and screwed together, stopped at one end by a fourth piece. Such a box greatly simplifies the production of a large number of pieces of wood exactly the same length and is well worth making if you are planning to include a staircase in your house.

(a) Making a cutting box

As you will need a large number of steps, it is worthwhile making a cutting box as wide as the depth of a single tread. Using a cutting box will ensure that the length of each tread will be the same. The box is made up of three pieces of wood glued and screwed together, with a fourth piece of wood fixed in one end to act as a stop. A vertical saw cut is made with a tenon saw at right-angles across the box and down to its base, in such a position that the distance from the end of the stop to the cut is exactly the length to which the stair treads must be cut (i.e. the width of a single flight of stairs). In Dickens' House this is $2\frac{3}{8}$ in. and the treads are cut from a piece of wood $1\frac{1}{4}$ in. wide and $\frac{1}{2}$ in. thick.

To cut the individual stair treads you push the wood strip into the cutting box from the open end until it is firmly against the closed end. Now place the tenon saw in the vertical cut you have made in the cutting box and saw right through the strip of wood inside. Repeat this operation until you have cut all the treads you need and you will have the satisfaction of seeing that they are all of equal length. It is quite a good idea to screw the cutting box firmly on to your work bench to hold it securely while you saw.

(b) Making an assembly box

Now is a good moment to construct what I call a general assembly box. It is only a part of a box really, just two pieces of wood glued and screwed together at right angles, these in turn being fixed to a plywood base. Make it accurately and you will find it invaluable for gluing pieces of wood together at a right-angle. If you put glossy paper between what you are gluing and the box, it will stop the two accidentally sticking together. To give you a guide to the size of the box, I suggest pieces 14 in. × 8 in. and 8 in. × 8 in. for the right-angle, and 15 in. × 8 in. for the base.

(c) Making a jig

Assembling the staircase is made much easier with a 'jig' specially constructed for the purpose. It takes a little time to make, but if you have several flights to make—as is the case in many houses—it is worth it. To make the jig for Dickens' House I used a strip of soft wood $1\frac{3}{4}$ in. wide and $\frac{1}{2}$ in. thick. It is important that the latter measurement is *exactly* the same as the thickness of the stair treads, as you will see in a moment. I started by cutting a piece $8\frac{1}{2}$ in. long and then cut more pieces, each $\frac{1}{2}$ in. shorter that the one before ($\frac{1}{2}$ in. because it is the distance from the front of one stair tread to the front of the next). When you have cut as many

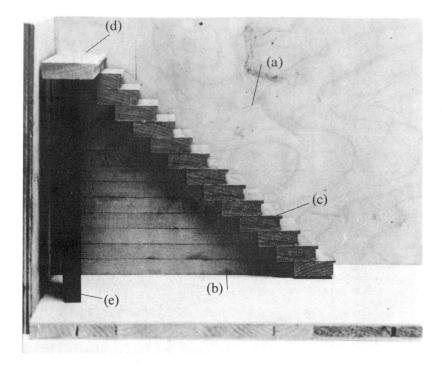

Each flight of stairs (c) is made by gluing one "tread" on top of another on the jig (b) which has been placed on the assembly box (a). Care must be taken to ensure that not too much glue is used as it is difficult to clean off once it has dried. Although the flights of stairs are of different lengths with a differing number of treads, this jig can still be used in the construction of all of them. The half-landing (d) which is shown at the top of this flight needs to be supported by a spare piece of wood (e) of the appropriate height as it dries.

pieces as there are stairs in the longest flight, place them one on top of the other, in the order you cut them, gluing them as you go. You can do the whole operation very easily in your assembly box. When the glue has set, cover all the steps of the jig with strips of Scotch tape, making sure that it fits snugly into the corners. The tape stops the glue you are going to use for sticking the treads together from sticking to the jig as well.

(d) Assembling the staircase

If you have decided to make a simple staircase you can now start by gluing the treads together, but if you want banisters turn to page 62 first, because these must be fitted before you glue the treads together. When you make the staircase, glue only the surfaces that overlap the assembly jig, and judge just the right amount of glue so that it does not spill over beyond the overlapping surfaces. Press each tread firmly on the one underneath until you have got the right number of treads in each flight of stairs. Allow each flight to set firmly on the jig before removing it. You will not need the whole of the jig for every flight of stairs; but it must be designed to enable you to make the longest flight.

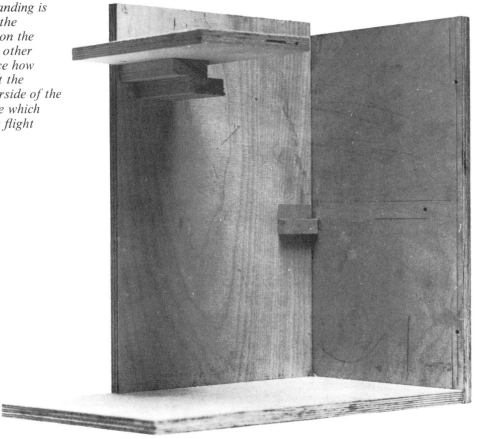

This "mock-up" shows how the half-landing is supported by a strip of wood glued to the central partition (there is also a strip on the inside of the house wall to support the other end, but this is not shown here). Notice how two treads are stuck together and that the higher one is also screwed to the underside of the floor above, in order to provide a ledge which will support the upper end of the short flight which goes up from the half-landing.

(e) Joining the flights to the half-landings

Next join the two long flights to their respective landings. The half-landings are made from pieces of wood the same thickness as the treads but slightly wider ($1\frac{1}{2}$ in.). Like the treads, they can be given a front lip. For Dickens' House you will need two of them, each $5\frac{7}{8}$ in. long. When you have cut them, glue one to the top of each long flight. Do this by resting the long flight on the staircase assembly jig, inside the assembly box, so that the top stair of the flight rests on the first step down. Cut an odd strip of wood so that its length is the same as the height of the assembly jig and use it to support the free end of the half-landing while the glue sets. The half-landing should be stuck in such a way as to make the top tread of the stair below the same depth as all the others. Repeat the operation for the other long flight of stairs.

The half-landings—and thus the lower flights—are each supported by two pieces of wood, one screwed to the central partition and another screwed at the same height immediately opposite it on the right-hand wall. I suggest wood of section $\frac{1}{2}$ in. $\times \frac{3}{16}$ in. for this purpose, and that the pieces for the partition and right-hand wall of Dickens' House be cut to lengths of $\frac{3}{4}$ in. and $1\frac{1}{2}$ in. respectively.

Alternatively (and more neatly) you can make slots about $\frac{1}{8}$ in. deep into which you can slide the half-landings (Fig. 1).

There is also a simple way to support the upper flights. Two extra treads are cut, stuck together on the assembly jig and then screwed to the underneath of the floor above. Slip a piece of thin card in between the floor and the treads. This will serve as packing, and make it easier to slip the stairs in and out when necessary. The flight is prevented from slipping backwards across the half-landing on which it rests by gluing a strip of wood (a piece left over from the window lining will do) under the bottom tread.

More realistic flights of stairs can be made by cutting off the back of each tread at 45°, either with a plane or putting them

Fig. 1

through a tilt-arbor circular-saw bench (Fig. 2). These are then stuck on a wooden base of the same width as the tread and about $\frac{1}{4}$ in. thick. Stick the top tread on first, about $\frac{1}{2}$ in. from one end of the base. When it is firmly stuck, add the others underneath each other (Figs 3 & 4).

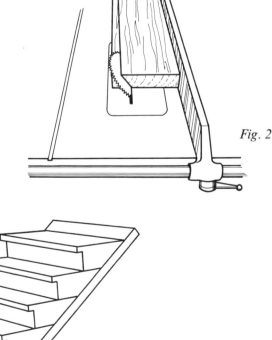

Fig. 2

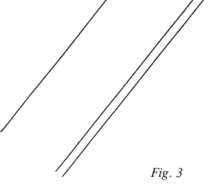

Fig. 3

Fig. 4

You can make a simple jig for gluing treads to the base by fixing two longer pieces of wood together at right angles (Fig. 5).

Fig. 5

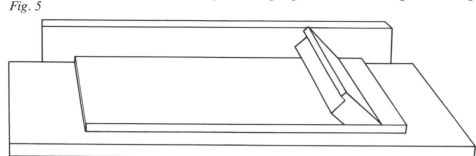

In the case of the longer flights, cut the bottom of the flight at 45°, to match the under surface of the bottom tread (Fig. 6). Then cut off the top end of the base at right angles, $\frac{1}{4}$ in. above the top tread (Fig. 4). This is now fitted into the half-landing by cutting a slot at 45° on the under surface of the landing into which the base is slid (Fig. 7).

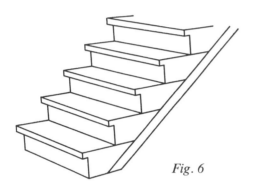

Fig. 6

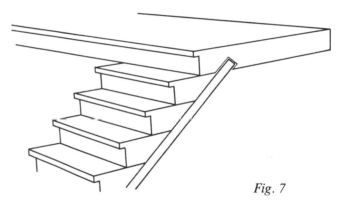

Fig. 7

The slot can be done with the tilt-arbor circular-saw bench.

In the case of the short flights, the top end of the base is cut level with the top tread, the bottom end is cut off at an angle of 45°. An extra tread is screwed on to the underside of the floor above, and you can now slide the short flight in sideways when it will be supported at the top and bottom as shown (Fig. 8).

The half-landings can be supported in the way described on pages 47 & 48. It is quite a good idea to delay fixing the floors until you know the exact height of the finished flights of stairs. Making the stairs to fit a predetermined floor height is difficult, it is easier to do it the other way round.

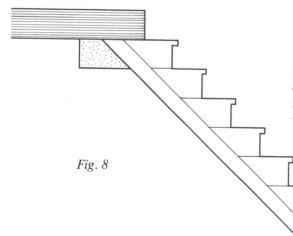

Fig. 8

The same "mock-up", showing the assembled staircase. Note that the bottom flight is placed in position first. The top end of the upper flight rests on the ledge screwed to the underside of the floor above, while the bottom end rests on the half-landing and is prevented from slipping across it by a small strip of wood which is glued to the underside of the bottom tread (arrowed).

3 Assembly

Sometimes when I make a dolls' house, I find it easier to do the interior decoration of the walls before putting it together. The design of Dickens' House presents no problems, for not only can the whole of the inside be taken out of the shell, but it can be taken to pieces merely by unslotting it. This could also be the case for any other house you make in accordance with the general principles given here. It is therefore safe to go ahead and make the shell from the parts you have already prepared and decorate them after assembly.

1. Assembling the shell

I suggest you use screws rather than nails, as the latter, though quicker to use, are easily driven in badly, can split the wood, bend if you are inexperienced and are difficult to withdraw if you have made a mistake. Start by marking where the screws are to be inserted. You have already drawn lines $\frac{3}{16}$ in. from the side edges of the top and bottom pieces. Now make three holes $\frac{3}{32}$ in. in diameter along these lines at the points indicated on your plans. Countersink them, so that the head of the screw sinks below the surface of the wood when it is screwed firmly in.

With the screw holes completed, fix the top to the sides. This is made much easier by temporarily tacking a strip of wood on to the underside of the top, to act as a 'stop', the thickness of the side away from the edge. When fixing these strips, do not bang the nails right down. Just hit them far enough to fix the strips of wood firmly, because you are going to remove them as soon as the shell is assembled. (If you want to avoid any nail holes in the ground floor, you can fix the strip using double-sided sticking tape, instead of nails.) Be very careful to put the sides the right way round: remember that in Dickens' House the left-hand side is the narrower one because it accommodates the hinge. Now, with the left-hand side of the top of the dolls' house resting on something

Use a hand-drill and countersink bit to make holes which will receive the heads of the screws used in assembling the shell. Protruding at the right-hand side is one of the "stops", the strips of wood which are temporarily tacked in position to ensure that the butting of the parts of the shell to one another is accurate.

of roughly similar height to the side piece, spread some glue on the top of the right-hand side and slip it under the top. Push it firmly against the 'stop' you have pinned underneath, and with a bradawl make a pilot hole for your first screw (see Appendix II for the correct size). Screw it home and repeat with the other two screws. Now rest the left-hand side of the top on top of the left side of the dolls' house and repeat the sequence. Carefully turn the pieces you have screwed together upside down and do the same with the base, ensuring the extra you have allowed as the 'street' protrudes at the front.

Then repeat the process with the back piece, this time using shorter screws (see Appendix II). Screw the back panel to the back of the base first, then to the sides, and finally to the top. Do not use any glue, for it may be useful to be able to remove the back at a later stage for decorating and fixing extra features such as those described in Part Five (Embellishments). Finally, pin and glue the strip of wood you made earlier (page 40) on to the front of the top of the house, with the widest side facing you. Fill all nail and screw holes with wood filler, allow it to dry and then rub down with sandpaper. The shell is now complete.

Screwing through the top and into the sides of the house. The strips of wood which act as "stops" will be removed as soon as assembly is complete.

Once the top has been fixed to the sides turn the house upside down to fix the base. Note that the plinth overlaps to act as a "street" over which the front door will swing. If a polished floor is going to be required in the hallway, the "stops" can be fixed with double-sided adhesive tape and removed without causing any damage to the floor.

When the back panel has been screwed in position (don't use any glue because you may well wish to remove it at a later date), the shell of the building is complete and requires only the addition of the top band of "stone work", which is shown in position here.

2. Fitting the front

As you know, a piano hinge is used to fix the front to the shell. You have already used part of it to hang the front door. Such hinges are available either in brass or in plated steel. Cut it to the required size with a hacksaw (you can, by the way, get a hacksaw blade suitable for the purpose that will fit into your padsaw handle). The hinge must be slightly shorter than the height of the front, and should be held firmly in a vice while you cut it. Having cut it, screw it to the back of the left-hand side of the front (refer to Appendix II again for the correct screw size) so that the pivot of the hinge projects beyond the edge of the wood. If you have got this right, the other side of the hinge should fit exactly over the front edge of the left-hand wall. Before you screw the hinge to this, lift the front up and slip a piece of card between it and the base of the house. This will ensure that the front swings easily over the 'street'. Do not put all the screws in at first, just in case you need to make adjustments and get it hanging properly. When you are satisfied that you have got it right, and all the screws have been inserted, add the hook and eye to the right side. Apart from decoration the outside is now complete.

53

When the shell assembly is complete the front can be screwed on, using a piano hinge.

Screw on a hook and eye to keep the front of the house closed.

4 Painting and decoration

1. Preparation

If you want a good finish to your work it is important to rub down the woodwork with sandpaper before painting it. Do this by wrapping a small sheet of sandpaper round a block of wood of a size which you can hold easily in your hand. Use the same grade as the one advised earlier (see Appendix II). Do not forget to sand the edges as well as the flat surfaces. Using a sandpapering block keeps these square and gives a professional finish.

Before starting to paint, make sure that the floors and partitions not only fit nicely together but, when assembled, slide easily in and out of the shell. If they are ill-fitting use a plane and sandpaper to make the necessary adjustments. If you have made the slots too narrow, enlarge them with sandpaper wrapped round a piece of wood slim enough to slip into the slot. The plane is used for reducing the outside edges and must be really sharp to cut the plywood cleanly. Always hold the wood firmly in a vice when planing or you will get very frustrated. Do not forget to check that the stairs fit properly and make any necessary adjustments with sandpaper.

2. Choosing the materials

The choice of decoration is a personal one, but to get a pleasing result it is better to stick to one period and work out a consistent theme. Avoid having too many changes of style and colour and remember that when you open the front you will immediately see all the interiors. Try for a harmonious overall scheme.

The choice of materials is the same as with ordinary house decoration. Plastic emulsion can be used direct on wood. It dries quickly, covers well and gives a semi-matt finish which suits small rooms. Paint with an eggshell finish is useful for outside work and doors—in fact for anything that is subject to a lot of handling. Remember to paint the window frames (I usually use white) before glazing. Many of you may have the necessary equipment to use cellulose paint. This gives the very best uniform, hard-wearing finish which will give your dolls' house a very professional look. The technique will not be described here, because if you have a spray gun, you will know how it is done. Where the wood in its natural state has an attractive colour or grain, the surface can be protected and the colour enriched by one of the polyurethane seals. Wallpaper has a particularly romantic appeal, especially if you can find papers with small floral designs. Lining the walls with silk gives a very rich and elegant appearance, which can be enhanced by the use of lighting.

The back of the front can pose a problem. If you try and match it with the scheme in each room you will end up with something that looks like a scrap album. If you decide to use wallpaper, which one do you choose? I think the safest way out of the dilemma is usually either to paint it a colour that blends with all the rooms or, as I did, use the most romantic of the wallpapers of those I had already selected for decorating the interior.

In general, when deciding on the scheme for Dickens' House, I tried to imagine what it would have looked like when Charles Dickens was in residence. It is not intended to be an authentic copy, (though devotees will recognise some items of furniture as being fairly exact copies of the original). The actual decoration was worked out in conjunction with my son, Dominic, and carried out by a friend who is a local painter and sign-writer of outstanding ability. He always does the painting first and then the wallpapering, and you would be well-advised to do the same. There are a considerable range of papers specially designed for dolls houses, as well as dolly papers of the Laura Ashley type. Sometimes you may find sheets of wrapping paper which can be very exciting.

Papering the back of the front needs careful forethought. To achieve a neat result, I find the most satisfactory method is to cut a sheet of wallpaper slightly larger than the whole of the back. Do this with a sharp knife with replaceable blades. Secure it temporarily with double-sided sticky tape, and then turn the front over and mark the position of the window and door openings with a pencil. Now remove the whole sheet from the back and cut out these openings (with the exception of the door), with a straight edge and a very sharp knife. After you have prepared your glazing materials (see 4. page 57), stick them in the window frames as described, and then paste the paper on the whole of the back of the front, making sure that the paper lines up in exactly the right position over the window openings. When the paper is really dry, cut off the excess around the outside and then cut out the door.

Because paper always expands when you wet it, apply the paste and allow it to stand for about 10 minutes, give it another brush over with paste and then stick it down. By doing this, it will contract as it dries and will thoroughly eliminate any wrinkles.

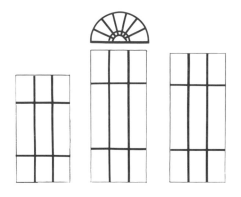

Make a drawing of each different sort of window to show where the additional sash bars are going to be placed. When the pieces of material (either glass, pvc or heavy plastic sheeting) with which you are going to "glaze" the windows have been cut to size, lay them over the master drawings. The, using the black lines which show through them to guide you, put the sash bars in, using either white or black adhesive tape or—if you have a steady hand—paint.

The use of plain glass in the windows and sash bars helps to give a really professional finish to the front of the house.

3. Floors and banisters

The floors and banisters (see page 62) can be sealed with polyurethane varnish and the stair treads painted white. The black and white 'tiles' in the hall in Dickens' House were made by laying down a sheet of white self-adhesive plastic first, and covering it with $\frac{3}{4}$ in. squares of the same material in black. You can purchase this sheeting in plain colours or in 'marbled' patterns. Hardwood flooring and glazed tiles are also available.

4. 'Glazing' the windows

Before you can regard the decoration of the front as complete, the windows have to be 'glazed'. There are various ways of doing this. Probably the simplest is to indicate the sash bars with strips of thin white adhesive plastic tape, which can be bought in reels, stuck on to sheets of clear heavy plastic or pvc. (The tape can be bought at the larger stationers, the plastic or pvc sheeting from do-it-yourself shops.) To ensure you put the sash bars in the right position, first make a drawing of the window opening on a sheet of paper and then indicate where the sash bars should be. This can be done quite effectively with a black felt pen. (If your drawing of the house front was fully detailed you will be able to use that.) Next, cut the plastic or pvc sheeting to a size that exactly fits the window opening. Place it symmetrically over your drawing and secure it in position with strips of ordinary sticky tape across the corners. Stick the white strips on the plastic sheeting or pvc in the positions indicated by your drawing. Repeat the process with all the window frames, remembering that the windows vary in size from floor to floor. You will need a special drawing for the fanlight over the front door.

A more realistic effect can be achieved by using thin glass and painting the sash bars on in white paint, but you should be warned that this needs a steady hand and a special brush, and ideally is undertaken by a sign-writer. If you want a truly authentic result you can represent all the sash bars in wood and use plain glass behind them.

If you have used plastic or pvc for the windows you can stick them to the backs of the frames with a clear adhesive. Use just enough around the edge of each sheet to make it stick without oozing out where it will be seen. If you have used glass, wait until the paint has dried really hard and then stick it into the back of the frame with a similar adhesive. Once the frames are dry you can paint them.

5. Decorating the exterior

The appearance of the outside of Dickens' House was, for me, dictated by the choice of subject, but you will probably have a freer hand. Why not have a look at some of the houses in your vicinity and find a colour scheme that appeals to you? Most towns and cities have plenty of unusual examples and in some cases house-owners have been very imaginative in their choice of colours. Alternatively, you might find something suitable in a book or magazine.

The front door can either be left natural and sealed with polyurethane, or stained and sealed, or painted. If you decide to paint it, either choose a colour which is in contrast to the rest of the front or paint it white to match the windows. It is as well to remove the 'furniture' (door handle and knocker) from the door before painting, otherwise it becomes a fiddly business. You can

The three partitions and the two floors are assembled and slid bodily into the completed shell.

58

give the house a number either by painting it on, or by using transfer lettering.

The rest of the outside of the house can be painted either the same as the front, or some natural colour like grey, white or sand. Where the ground floor projects beyond the front, I usually paint it grey to represent the street outside, or leave it unpainted and sealed with polyurethane varnish.

A view of the assembled house from the back, prior to decorating. The back panel has not yet been screwed on and you can see quite clearly how the half-landings are supported.

6. Final assembly

Wait until the paint is dry and then slot the interior together, as on page 59. It is quite a good idea to fix the central partition to the side partition with two screws. One at the top and one at the bottom of each side partitions. Slide it carefully into the shell, and when it is properly in, put the long staircase flights in position, resting the half-landings on the supports or slide them into the slots (see page 48) on either side of the staircase well. Slide the short flights in sideways from right to left, with the top flight resting on the ledge under the ceiling and the bottom resting on the half-landing. If you have added banisters, you will not be able to put the flights rising from the half-landings in in this way, and you will either have to slip them in from the back of the house by removing the back panel, or pull the skeleton forwards, leaving the half-landing behind, and insert the short flight in position before sliding the skeleton back in again.

Front elevation for
Dickens' House model
Reduced facsimile (30%)

61

5 Embellishments

There is a distinction to be drawn between complex design and embellishment. A complex design must be more difficult to achieve and to construct than a simple one, but embellishments are usually for the most part uncomplicated and require only additional time and materials for their completion.

The methods described in this book so far are those which I feel will enable you to build simply a very satisfying dolls' house either to a design of your own choosing or, by copying the detailed instructions, based on Dickens' House. Any little girl will probably be very glad to have it. However, should you share my desire to indulge in even greater realism, you may wish to embellish—not complicate—the basic design. Let us consider the additional possibilities under the following headings: Banisters, Curtains, Doors, Wall fittings and Lighting.

1. Banisters

To make these more elaborate, you must turn back to page 48 and work on the treads before sticking them together, drilling holes for a banister in the top of each tread. Banisters can be made of metal or of wood.

(a) Wooden

If you are using wood, I suggest either $\frac{1}{8}$ in. square section or $\frac{1}{8}$ in. diameter dowel. If the banisters are made of square section wood, you will find that you can tap them gently into the drill holes with a light hammer to give a good snug fit. Experiment with an odd piece of wood until you get the right size of drill.

Use the stair-cutting jig to get the wooden banisters all the same length (you will need to make another cut for the saw to fix the length) and then make a drilling jig to ensure that the holes occupy the same place on all the treads. To do this, nail two pieces of wood the same thickness as the treads at right-angles on to a third flat piece of wood. Decide where you want the hole in the first tread and drill it out. Now drill a hole of similar size through

This drilling jig ensures that the hole made to receive the banisters on each tread of the stairs is in exactly the same position and drilled to the same depth.

Using the drilling jig to make a hole in one tread for a banister. Note the drill stop which ensures a constant depth of hole.

another piece of wood and nail this piece over the right-angle you have made, in such a way that its hole and the hole in the tread line up together when the tread is pushed into the right-angle. You can now remove the first tread from the drilling jig and insert another one. Using the fixed hole as a guide, you can drill all the other treads, confident that the hole in each will be in exactly the right position. You can make the depth of the hole in all the treads constant by gluing immediately next to the hole a block of wood of such a height that it acts as a shoulder and stops the chuck of the drill at the same point each time. Next glue in the banisters and then glue the treads together as described on page 46.

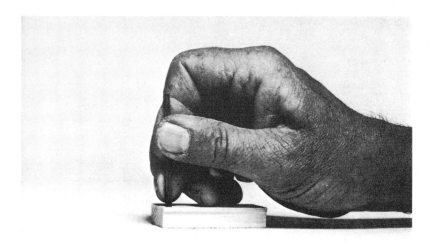

When the banisters have been cut to length place one in each tread before assembling the treads on the assembly jig.

Join them all together at their top end with a wooden hand-rail. This can be most easily prepared by running a piece of wood $\frac{1}{4}$ in. square over a circular saw so that a channel $\frac{1}{8}$ in. deep is cut into one side. Alternatively, it can be composed from one strip of wood, of the same thickness as an individual banister, flanked on each side by a thin strip to form a channel for the banisters. Whichever method you use, the hand-rail must be shaped with a wooden rasp or sandpaper before it is fitted to the banisters. Each hand-rail should project beyond the first and last banister by about $\frac{3}{8}$ in. Mark out what the final length of the rail should be, then cut it and fill in the ends of the channel with short lengths of banister wood so that it looks solid from the ends. Round off the ends of the hand-rail and glue on to the banisters, making sure that the latter are vertical and parallel to each other. Use elastic bands to ensure a close fit while the glue is setting.

If you are making stairs in the alternative way described on pages 48 and 49, Fig. 9 shows you how the banisters would look.

(b) Brass

Banisters made in brass can look very elegant, but you need some experience in soldering to get good results. Start, as before, by making in each tread a hole the same diameter as the brass rod you are going to use as a banister. You will need a cutting jig to help you clip these to the same length. This is made simply by

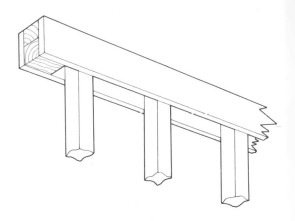

A diagrammatic enlargement of one way of constructing the hand-rail if you have no access to a circular saw. The top is flanked on each side by a thin strip to form a channel the same width as the banisters. When this has been cut to length the ends are stopped with pieces of banister wood to make it look solid.

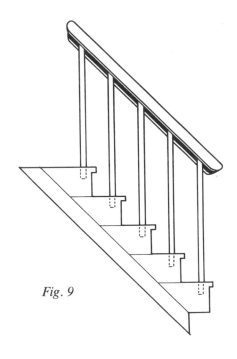

Fig. 9

The hand-rail must be rounded and smoothed on its top edges and at the ends before it is glued on to the tops of the banisters. Elastic bands hold it in position until the glue sets.

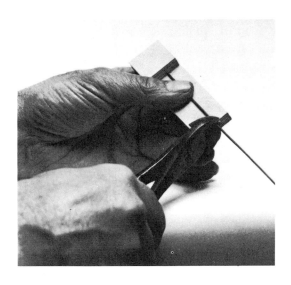

Brazing rods being cut to length on a cutting jig to ensure that they are all the same length.

pinning a wooden 'stop' piece on to another piece of wood so that the distance from the edge of the wood to the stop is the length of the banister. I find that $\frac{3}{32}$ in. diameter brazing rods make excellent banisters. Using wire-shears, cut the required number of banisters, tap them into their holes in the treads and then glue the treads together on the staircase assembly jig.

The hand-rail is made either from flat strip or half-round brass. The latter looks more realistic, but you may not be able to find any. A model-makers' shop, or your local scrap-metal merchant, should be able to help you here. Before soldering the rail on to the banisters, make a whorl at either end with round-nosed pliers. You will find this relatively easy with flat brass strip, but almost impossible with the thicker half-round section, so if you are using this just turn the ends down and round them off.

Soldering the rail to the banisters needs patience and a steady hand, but it looks very satisfying when completed. Finish it off with steel wool to give it a nice bright look, and then seal it with polyurethane matt varnish to delay tarnishing. If you want to be really ambitious, you can stick the two flights of stairs together by means of the half-landing, having first drilled a hole in it for an extra banister. This extra one will have to be longer than the rest

This mock-up of the staircase shows the brass balustrade in position. The hand-rail, which appears continuous, is made from several sections soldered together.

of the banisters and is not cut to length until the continuous hand-rail is fitted. The latter has to be done in sections as it is difficult to bend the rail tightly enough to get round the corners in one. Solder the individual sections together, having butted them up to one another as neatly as possible. (*Note*: If you make a continuous hand-rail you will have to insert the completed staircase from the rear of the house, having first removed the back panel.)

2. Curtains

Turning now to the rooms themselves, you can produce very realistic effects from quite simple additions. Start with the curtains. Heavy Victorian curtain rails can be simulated by using $\frac{1}{4}$ in. diameter dowel cut to length and then drilled out with a very fine drill so that you can insert a large-headed upholstery tack into the end without splitting it. The dowel can then be stained to represent mahogany, or painted white. The curtain rail can be held up with screw eyes of a suitable size, inserted either side of the window opening or room arch for which the curtain is intended. You can have the curtain rails either in front of or behind an arch; either way is attractive. You can also buy ready-made curtain rails in brass.

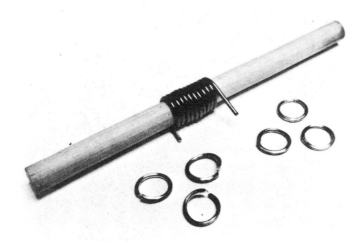

Curtain rings are easily made. A piece of copper wire is wound round a section of dowelling. The wire is then removed from the dowel and the rings are completed by soldering the ends together.

The curtains look well with minute rings sewn to them, or hemmed to accept the dowel. The rings are made by wrapping copper wire around a piece of dowel and cutting off complete circles from the spiral. Each circle is then flattened and its ends soldered together. The finished result is very effective but, as with all top-class model making, it requires time and patience.

To finish off the curtains, you can loop them back with gold string (similar to that used for tying up Christmas parcels) and a tassel can be made by teasing out the end of the string. Use a small screw eye behind the curtain to fix the string to the wall.

3. Doors

The doors themselves are easily made from $\frac{1}{4}$ in. plywood. There are two ways of hanging them. One is with tiny hinges, which should be let into the side of the door to avoid having too big a gap between the door and its frame. Fix the hinges either with pins or with very fine screws. You can give additional strength to the fixing by using one of the epoxy resin glues as well.

The other way of hinging is to make two short cuts on one side of the door and two matching cuts in the door frame. Cut two small strips of hard plastic sheeting to act as a bridge between the slots and insert them in the door. Next drill a fine hole at each end, one from the top and one from the bottom of the door so that the drill passes through the plastic strip. Take the drill out and replace it with a panel pin. The door will now hinge on the plastic strips. Using epoxy resin, glue the free ends and push them into the slots in the door frame.

You can make more elaborate doors and door frames if you wish. To make the frames, start off with lengths of wood $\frac{5}{8}$ in. square. On one side cut a groove $\frac{1}{8}$ in. deep and as wide as the thickness of the wall (usually $\frac{3}{8}$ in.) which is to be inserted into it.

Examples of two methods of hinging doors. On the left, the "hinges" are made from pieces of hard plastic sheeting. One end of each hinge is secured in a saw-cut made in the door. It is then pinned from either the top or bottom of the door so that it is held permanently in position but allowed to swivel. The other end is then glued into a saw-cut made in the door frame itself. The door on the right has been hung on small conventional hinges.

On the opposite side cut a rebate $\frac{1}{8}$ in. deep and $\frac{1}{2}$ in. wide (Fig. 10). Ideally this is done with a router, but it can be done with a rabbeting plane. Next cut the lengths of prepared wood to the required size, but remember that the dimensions of the door frames will be slightly larger than those of the door opening. Mitre the corners at the top and trim off any excess at the bottom so that the whole frame fits snugly to the door opening (Fig 11).

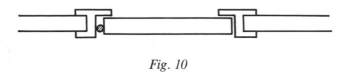

Fig. 10

A third method of hinging the doors, using the door frames, is to glue a small diameter dowel down one edge of the door, projecting slightly at both ends, and to fit the dowel into holes (of the same diameter as the dowel) drilled into the door frame at the top and into a thin board forming a threshold at the bottom (Figs 10 & 11). The threshold also ensures that the door will ride over floor coverings, especially carpets and tiles, when it opens. If you want to remove the door for decorating, this can be achieved by making the threshold a tight fit so that it can be slid out of the frame and with it, the door.

More elaborate panelled doors are not too difficult to make. First make a full size drawing of the door you would like to make. Use $\frac{1}{4}$ in. thick wood (hardwood like mahogany for your grand doors; softwood for bedroom doors etc.) and, as you will need pieces of varying width for the stiles, panels and rails, run off a number of lengths of each width. These can then be cut to the appropriate length (use a cutting box, page 44, to achieve this accurately). Now cut the styles slightly longer than the finished height of the door. Chamfer all the edges of the panels with sandpaper and then glue all the pieces together at once. Clamp the assembled door together whilst the glue sets. Trim off the projecting sides of the stiles and the door is ready to hinge.

Inexpensive ear studs make very elegant door knobs. First make a hole in the door with a very fine drill and then push the stud into the hole, using the same adhesive to stick it firmly in position. You can also buy ready-made door knobs in brass.

Fig. 11

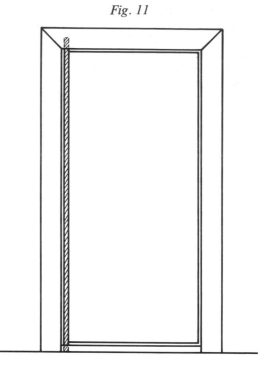

Examples of panelled doors

This suggests some ideas how you can set about decorating the wainscoting, picture rails, architrave and skirting board. Plugs and sockets of a suitable size can be obtained from a variety of stockists. The one in the picture was from a hearing aid. Note also the use of a gilt ear stud as a door handle.

4. Wall fittings

Wainscoting, skirting boards, architraves and picture rails can all be simulated by selecting wood of suitable shape and sticking it to the walls. Suitable wooden mouldings of all shapes are available from stockists. If you do this in the front rooms you will not be able to take out the inside of the house from the front, and that is why I have suggested that you leave the back unglued. Avoid gluing these additions together at the corners, or you will not be able to take the partitions apart or extract the inside of the house from its shell at all. If you are going to use wallpapers, remember that these other features must be painted, stained or polished first.

69

5. Lighting

There is not the slightest doubt that artificial lighting enhances an interior, especially if it is richly furnished. Electricity from the household mains is the ideal source of power, using a transformer to reduce the voltage to a suitable level. The alternative to a transformer is dry (or wet) batteries. The latter are heavy and need re-charging, but the former have a short life and cause corrosion if they are not removed when spent.

(a) Transformers

Lighting systems using 12 volt bulbs seem to be the most popular today, though there is still a small demand for transformers with an output of 3.5 volts. Make sure the output in amps is adequate. Determine this by multiplying the amperage of the individual light bulb, by the number of lights you intend to use in the dolls' house. The result gives you a figure called VA, and that is the output you will need from your transformer. The transformer itself **must conform to the country's safety standards.** There are two basic types: one forming part of the mains plug, the other a separate unit that is connected by wires to the mains plug. The former is the most convenient, the safest, and comes with output wires that can be connected directly to your dolls' house lighting system.

(b) Wiring

There are two ways of wiring up your lights: one is in series, the other is in parallel. The latter is the one to use, because with the former, if one bulb fails, all the others go out. Fig. 12 shows how to connect lights in parallel.

When you come to install the wiring, you can either copy the method used in ordinary household wiring, with the wires buried in the walls and ceilings, or you can use thin copper tape stuck onto the walls with its own adhesive. The former, using old insulated telephone wires, is cheaper, but you have to make grooves in the wall to hide them. Copper tape is easier to use, but more expensive. The former gives you a better finish when you come to do the wall-papering.

To find out where to cut the grooves, work out a complete wiring plan for each component of the interior. You may like to have pendants from the ceilings as well as, or instead of, wall lights. The same principles will apply in fixing these.

Having made your wiring plans, cut the grooves. It is helpful to tack a piece of wood alongside the line of the groove if you are using a handsaw, as it makes it easier to keep the saw in the right position. The groove should only go half way through the thickness of the wood. See photo page 71. The grooves can also be cut very neatly with a router, but this is an expensive tool.

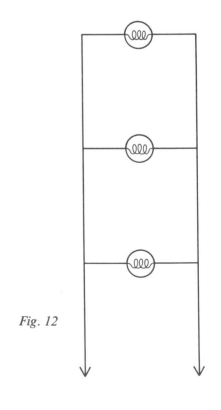

Fig. 12

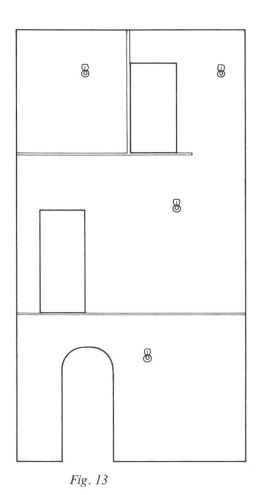

Fig. 13

When you come to connect the wires or tape to the light fitting, try and arrange for the light fitting to be on the opposite side of the wall to the groove (Fig. 13). Drill a hole in the wall where you want your light fitting and then paper the wall on the side on which you want to fix your light fitting.

When the paper is properly dry, thread the wires from the light fitting through the hole and stick the light fitting to the wallpaper. Now connect these wires to the supply wires with solder and then paper the grooved side of the wall. Secure the supply wires in the grooves with selotape whilst papering (Fig. 14).

There are various ways of connecting lamps to the copper tape, depending on the make, but the principle is the same: eyelets or pins pushed through the tape and the lamps connected to these.

When you come to assemble the partitions and floors, I suggest you use the central partition as the collecting point for your wiring. Wires from the side partitions and floors can be plugged into it, as can the main electricity supply (small scale plugs and sockets are obtainable for this purpose). This only applies when the floors and partitions are made to be removed for ease of decoration etc., as in most of my dolls' houses.

(c) Light fittings

Grain of wheat bulbs are now the most widely used in dolls' house light fittings. They consist of a small glass bulb with two wires coming from it which are soldered to the supply wires (or

Note: Figs 13 and 14 are diagrammatic and do not relate specifically to the Dickens' House.

If the electrical wiring is to be concealed it is necessary to cut grooves in the walls and floors of the house with a saw. Tacking a piece of wood alongside the line of the groove will help you saw a straight line.

inserted into miniature plugs and sockets). These have a very long life, but when they burn out, the whole fitting has to be sent back to the manufacturer. This is not a problem, if you chose light fittings with miniature Edison Screw bulbs, which are very easy to replace and in the correct scale.

You can also use the small plugs and sockets for standard lamps, table lamps and flickering five units, as well as strings of minute Christmas tree lights.

(d) Connection to the power supply

The ideal place to bring in your power supply is at the bottom of the dolls house, at the back. If you are using a combined plug and transformer, the supply wires will be at a low voltage and can be connected directly to the dolls' house wiring. If the transformer and mains plug are separate, the power supply will be at mains voltage, and will go straight to the transformer, inside the dolls' house, hidden conveniently under stairs or in the roof. The output from this can be connected anywhere to the dolls' house wiring.

The combined transformer and mains plug is the safer system where young children are concerned. If a separate transformer is fitted inside the dolls' house it is recommended that a BSI approved circuit breaker is fitted to the main supply socket.

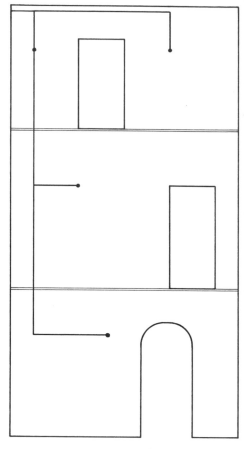

Fig. 14

6 Making a pitched or sloping roof

When our forebears designed a roof they had to give it a sharp slope so that the rain would quickly run off the straw which was in common use as a roofing material. Nowadays it is possible to make a house watertight with a completely flat roof so we are free to choose from a variety of shapes. Inevitably, the roof with a high pitch looks more romantic but is more difficult to make than one where the sides are at right-angles:

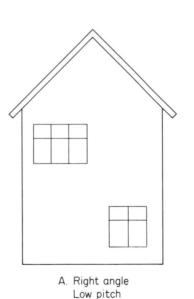

A. Right angle
Low pitch

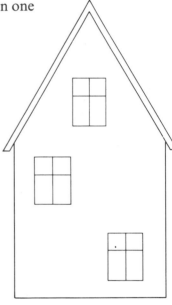

B. Acute angle
High pitch

This is because in **A**, where the two sides meet at the top or ridge, there is a straightforward right-angle joint whereas in **B** the edges have to be shaped to an acute angle (place the wood in a vice to do this and shape it with a plane):

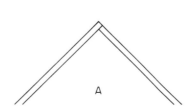

A   B

Don't try and do this:

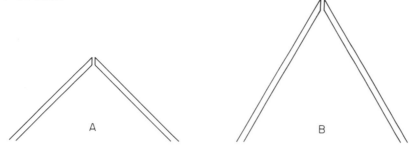

because it is very difficult to get a neat joint this way. When you are drawing the sides of the house (known as the "gable end"), first of all draw a line down the centre, decide how high you want the front and back walls and then mark off the sloping lines:

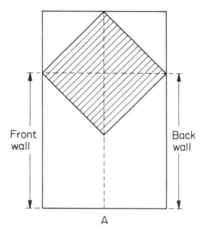

If you want a roof with a higher pitch, cut the card accordingly:

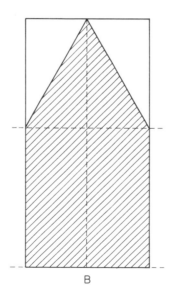

After drawing out the gable end, cut it out and then use it as a template for marking out the other end.

When it comes to cutting the roof sides, you can either leave the lower edges square or you can trim them with a plane to form a "soffit":

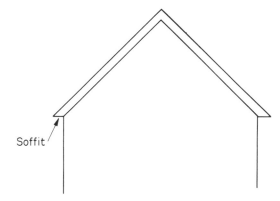

Soffit

Likewise you can either leave the top of the walls square or trimmed to an angle to make a close fit under the roof:

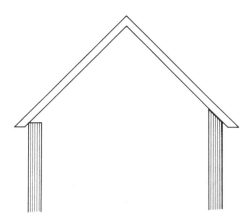

Afterword

If you have read this book straight through, you may have the impression that it is all rather complicated, particularly if you have done very little or no woodworking before. I can assure you that in practice it really is not so. Taken step by step it is both worthwhile and enjoyable. Indeed, if you get half as much satisfaction from building a dolls' house as I do, and from seeing a child play with it afterwards, you will be amply rewarded.

May I offer one final thought? Whenever you are tempted to rush any part of the job, remember that in all probability what you are building will not only be played with by the child you have it in mind for at present, but also children of generations yet unborn. For, despite all the technological advances of our times, there is undoubtedly still a place for craftsmanship, and a dolls' house carefully made by hand today is almost certain in due course to become justly prized as an heirloom.

For the future

I hope the next stage in reproducing real life in the dolls' house will be the provision of a working plumbing system with running water and drains.

Appendix I

List of tools and their uses

These can be obtained from any good hardware store.

Essential tools

Rip saw, sawing plywood sheets into suitable shapes
Tenon saw, used with woodcutting jigs
Pad saw, cutting openings in the interior of a sheet of wood
Fret saw, a thin, fine-toothed saw for cutting curved shapes and for cutting openings in the interior of a sheet of wood
Hacksaw blade, to fit in the pad saw when cutting metal
Hobbyknife, cutting thin, light materials
Brace, holding centre bit or drill for making holes
Countersink bit, making a bevelled cup in the wood to receive the head of a screw
Centre bit ($\frac{5}{8}$ in. diam.), making larger holes

Twist drill ($\frac{1}{8}$ in. diam.), making holes for screws
Hand drill, general-purpose drill for smaller holes
Bradawl, making small holes in wood, especially for screws
Nail punch (nail set), used with a hammer to sink nail-heads below wood surface
Small vice, to hold wood firmly while drilling, sawing or planing
Smoothing plane, smoothing edges cut by saw
Hammer
Screwdriver
Pencil, compass, india-rubber (eraser), ruler, set square, making the preparatory drawings and drawing the cutting lines on wood

Non-essential tools

Woodworking bench, general use
Sawing stool, sawing at knee level
T-square, marking out, especially parallel lines
Circular-saw bench, cutting wood mechanically etc.
Rabbeting plane, making steps and channels in wood
Wire-cutters, round-nosed pliers, making metal banisters
Soldering iron, solder and flux, joining pieces of metal, electric wiring, joints etc.

Fine twist drill ($\frac{1}{32}$ in. diam.), inserting upholstery tacks in end of dowelling to simulate curtain rods
Electric jig saw, cutting shapes in the middle of a sheet of wood (an easier way of doing what a pad saw will do for you)
Electric router, cutting grooves in wood as well as doing all the things a jig saw will do. A very expensive tool.

N.B. For expensive woodworking machinery it is worth consulting an expert firm.

Appendix II

Materials used in making Dolls' Houses

Most of the materials listed below are obtainable from any good do-it-yourself shop or from stationers

Birch plywood, main structure inside and out
M.D.F. (Medium Density Fibreboard), as an alternative to plywood, easier to shape, does not warp, takes paint well
Soft wood, window sills, plinths, staircase etc.
Hardboard, arches
Balsa wood, window linings
Thick card, door panels
Sandpaper (80 grit), smoothing wood
Woodworking glue
Panel pins, ($\frac{1}{2}$ in.) pinning plinths etc. on front
Piano hinge (3 ft × 1 in.)
Screws ($\frac{3}{8}$ in.) No. 4 countersunk brass, for hinges
  ($\frac{5}{8}$ in.) No. 4 countersunk brass, screwing on back
  ($\frac{3}{4}$ in.) No. 4 countersunk brass, general assembly
Screw-eye and split-ring ($\frac{3}{8}$ in. diam.), door knocker
Brass drawer knob or large rivet, door knob
Scotch tape
Double-sided adhesive tape, useful for sticking two pieces of wood together temporarily
Hook and eye (1 in.), fastening front of dolls' house to body
Wood filler

For decoration

Plastic emulsion
Egg-shell finish paint
Polyurethane seal
Wallpaper
Silk, wall linings
Plastic sheeting, imitation stone or marble floors
Cellulose paint if you have a spray gun

For windows

White adhesive plastic tape in reels, representing sash bars
Heavy plastic or pvc sheeting, representing glass
Black felt pen, to draw out sash bars on a sheet of paper
Thin glass, as an alternative to the plastic or pvc
Sable paint brush, lining out sash bars with paint
Clear adhesive, for fixing glass windows, acetate or pvc sheet windows

Staircases

Elastic bands, to hold hand-rail on banisters while glue is setting
Brass brazing rod ($\frac{3}{32}$ in. diam.), brass banisters
Flat or half-round brass strip ($\frac{1}{8}$ in. wide), brass hand-rails
Steel wool, polishing metal

Doors

Small hinges (about $\frac{1}{2}$ in. long)
Hard plastic sheet, making hinges
Epoxy resin glue, sticking hinges
Ear studs, door knobs

Electricals

Transformers
Insulated wire
Electrical connectors
Miniature switches

Appendix III

Wood-cutting list for Dickens' House

Part	Measurements in Inches
Birch plywood	
Front	$29\frac{1}{8} \times 17\frac{1}{2} \times \frac{3}{8}$
Front door	$6\frac{1}{2} \times 3\frac{1}{2} \times \frac{3}{8}$
Hinge piece	$6\frac{1}{2} \times \frac{3}{8} \times \frac{3}{8}$
Gauge pieces for gluing central sash bars	
top windows	$2\frac{5}{8}$ ⎫ Width and
middle windows	$3\frac{1}{4}$ ⎬ thickness not
bottom windows	$3\frac{1}{8}$ ⎭ important
Top	$17\frac{1}{2} \times 16\frac{1}{8} \times \frac{3}{8}$
Base	$19\frac{1}{4} \times 17\frac{1}{2} \times \frac{3}{8}$
Left side	$29\frac{1}{8} \times 15\frac{5}{8} \times \frac{3}{8}$
Right side	$29\frac{1}{8} \times 15\frac{3}{4} \times \frac{3}{8}$
Left partition	$29\frac{1}{8} \times 10\frac{1}{2} \times \frac{3}{8}$
Right partition	$29\frac{1}{8} \times 5\frac{7}{8} \times \frac{3}{8}$
Centre partition	$29\frac{1}{8} \times 15\frac{3}{4} \times \frac{3}{8}$
First floor	$16\frac{3}{4} \times 15\frac{3}{4} \times \frac{3}{8}$
Second floor	$16\frac{3}{4} \times 15\frac{3}{4} \times \frac{3}{8}$
General assembly box	14×8 ⎫
	8×8 ⎬ Thickness
	15×8 ⎬ at least $\frac{3}{8}$
Support for fretsawing	12×8 ⎭
Back	$29\frac{7}{8} \times 17\frac{1}{2} \times \frac{1}{4}$
Hardboard	
Arch at front door	$12 \times 8 \times \frac{1}{8}$

Part	Measurements in Inches
Soft wood	
Top band for front	$17\frac{1}{2} \times \frac{5}{16} \times \frac{3}{16}$
Band below first-floor windows	$17\frac{1}{2} \times \frac{7}{16} \times \frac{3}{16}$
Window sills (5 needed)	$3\frac{3}{16} \times \frac{5}{16} \times \frac{3}{16}$
Band on front of roof	$17\frac{1}{2} \times \frac{3}{4} \times \frac{3}{8}$
Plinth at bottom of front	$17\frac{1}{2} \times \frac{5}{16} \times \frac{5}{16}$
Staircase treads (39 needed)	$2\frac{3}{8} \times 1\frac{1}{4} \times \frac{1}{2}$
Wood for staircase jig	$78 \times 1\frac{3}{4} \times \frac{1}{2}$
Half landings (2 needed)	$5\frac{7}{8} \times 1\frac{1}{2} \times \frac{1}{2}$
Supports for half landings	
(2 needed)	$\frac{3}{4} \times \frac{1}{2} \times \frac{3}{16}$
(2 needed)	$1\frac{1}{2} \times \frac{1}{2} \times \frac{3}{16}$
Soft wood or balsa wood	
Window linings	$14 \text{ ft} \times \frac{1}{8} \times \frac{1}{8}$
Lips for staircase treads	$9 \text{ ft} \times \frac{1}{16} \times \frac{1}{16}$
2-ply or thick card	
Door panels	
(2 needed)	$\frac{3}{4} \times \frac{3}{4} \times \frac{3}{32}$
(4 needed)	$1\frac{3}{4} \times \frac{3}{4} \times \frac{3}{32}$

Metric conversion table

Inches	Milli-metres	Inches	Milli-metres	Inches	Milli-metres	Inches	Milli-metres	Inches	Milli-metres
$\frac{1}{16}$	1.6	$\frac{1}{2}$	12.7	$\frac{15}{16}$	23.8	7	177.8	20	508.0
$\frac{1}{8}$	3.2	$\frac{9}{16}$	14.3	1	25.4	8	203.2	30	762.0
$\frac{3}{16}$	4.8	$\frac{5}{8}$	15.9	2	50.8	9	228.6	40	1016.0
$\frac{1}{4}$	6.4	$\frac{11}{16}$	17.5	3	76.2	10	254.0	50	1270.0
$\frac{5}{16}$	7.9	$\frac{3}{4}$	19.1	4	101.6	11	279.4	75	1905.0
$\frac{3}{8}$	9.5	$\frac{13}{16}$	20.7	5	127.0	12	304.8	100	2540.0
$\frac{7}{16}$	11.1	$\frac{7}{8}$	22.2	6	152.4	15	381.0		

Appendix IV

Stockists

Wood products

Medium Density Fibreboard (M.D.F.)
Birch Plywood
  From major Wood Merchants—e.g. Jewsons
All types of Mouldings, Staircases, Doors, Windows
etc.
  From Borcraft Miniatures
      Scotland Lane,
      Horsforth,
      Leeds,
      W. Yorks. LS18 5SZ.

  From Hobby's
      Knight's Hill Square,
      London, SE27 0HH.

Ceramic Building Materials

Bricks, Tiles, etc.
  From Terry Curran,
      27 Chapel Street,
      Mosborough,
      Nr Sheffield,
      S. Yorks. S19 5BT.

Electricals

  From Hobby's—*as above*.

  From Wood N. Wool Miniatures
      3 Stankelt Road,
      Silverdale,
      Carnforth,
      Lancs. LA5 0RB.

Transformers
  From Longbarn Enterprises,
      Low Mill,
      Bainbridge,
      Leyburn,
      N. Yorks. DL8 3EF.

From Blackwells
      733 Loudon Road,
      Westcliffe on Sea,
      Essex SS0 9ST.

Door Furniture

  From G. Bailey,
      131 Centre Drive,
      Newmarket,
      Suffolk.